DO Drops

Volume 4

DO Drops

Volume 4

Daily Bible Devotional

Dr. Bo Wagner

Word of His Mouth Publishers
Mooresboro, NC

All Scripture quotations are taken from the **King James Version** of the Bible.

ISBN: 978-1-941039-14-4
Printed in the United States of America
©2020 Dr. Bo Wagner (Robert Arthur Wagner)

Word of His Mouth Publishers
Mooresboro, NC 28114
www.wordofhismouth.com

Cover art by Chip Nuhrah

Devotion 01

Saul was dead, but the news of that would not reach David in Ziklag for a couple of days. When it did, it was brought by a man who hoped to gain favor with David, whom he rightly surmised would be the next King of Israel. And what better way to gain favor with David, he thought, than to portray himself as the one who killed his enemies?

2 Samuel 1:5 *And David said unto the young man that told him, How knowest thou that Saul and Jonathan his son be dead?* **6** *And the young man that told him said, As I happened by chance upon mount Gilboa, behold, Saul leaned upon his spear; and, lo, the chariots and horsemen followed hard after him.* **7** *And when he looked behind him, he saw me, and called unto me. And I answered, Here am I.* **8** *And he said unto me, Who art thou? And I answered him, I am an Amalekite.* **9** *He said unto me again, Stand, I pray thee, upon me, and slay me: for anguish is come upon me, because my life is yet whole in me.* **10** *So I stood upon him, and slew him, because I was sure that he could not live after that he was fallen: and I took the crown that was upon his head, and the bracelet that was on his arm, and have brought them hither unto my lord.*

If you are comparing in your mind the account that this man gave with the account that we find in 1 Samuel 31, you notice that the accounts do not match. Simply put, this man was lying. Saul was dead by the time he arrived, and this man simply took his crown and bracelet. Then he brought those things to David as "proof" of what he was saying. He evidently expected David to celebrate and to reward him for what he had done.

Instead, David had the man killed:

1 Samuel 1:14 *And David said unto him, How wast thou not afraid to stretch forth thine hand to destroy the LORD'S anointed? 15 And David called one of the young men, and said, Go near, and fall upon him. And he smote him that he died. 16 And David said unto him, Thy blood be upon thy head; for thy mouth hath testified against thee, saying, I have slain the LORD'S anointed.*

Lying got this man killed. Had he told the truth, he would not have "gained the glory" he sought, but he would have walked away alive! DO meditate on the fact that because God hates lying lips, He has built-in consequences in every situation for those that lie. So, DO tell the truth!

Personal Notes:

_____

_____

_____

_____

_____

_____

_____

_____

_____

_____

_____

_____

_____

_____

_____

Devotion 02

Upon hearing that Saul and his sons were dead, David rent his clothes in anguish, and all of his men did so as well. Then they fasted and wept and mourned for them the rest of the day. If that sounds surprising, given how many times Saul tried to murder David, it only gets more surprising as the text goes on:

2 Samuel 1:19 *The beauty of Israel is slain upon thy high places: how are the mighty fallen!*

2 Samuel 1:22 *From the blood of the slain, from the fat of the mighty, the bow of Jonathan turned not back, and the sword of Saul returned not empty.* **23** *Saul and Jonathan were lovely and pleasant in their lives, and in their death they were not divided: they were swifter than eagles, they were stronger than lions.* **24** *Ye daughters of Israel, weep over Saul, who clothed you in scarlet, with other delights, who put on ornaments of gold upon your apparel.*

2 Samuel 1:27 *How are the mighty fallen, and the weapons of war perished!*

Saul was lovely and pleasant in his life? Weep over Saul? It makes a person want to ask, "Are we talking about the same person?"

Saul was miserable and petty and hateful to David, and yet, upon his death, David mentioned none of that at all. Instead, he chose only to mention the good things in the life of Saul. That is called graciousness and respect for the dead. And it is all but gone in our world today. Recently a man died of cancer. He was a man who gave heavily to conservative political causes, but also gave hundreds of millions to medical research to find cures for childhood diseases. When he died, a truly despicable human being, "comedian" Bill Maher, said, "I'm glad he's dead, and I hope the end was painful."

This kind of sewer level behavior is what society comes to when they cast aside things like graciousness and respect for the dead. If anyone had a right to say, "I'm glad he's dead, and I hope the end was painful," it was David. And yet he spoke well of the dead instead, rightly acknowledging that Saul did a great many wonderful things for the nation, despite his animosity toward David.

DO be fair, gracious, and as respectful as possible to the dead, especially when others have many reasons to love them. One day you will be the one being eulogized, and you would want the same treatment!

Personal Notes:

_____

_____

_____

_____

_____

_____

_____

_____

_____

_____

_____

_____

_____

_____

_____

Devotion 03

With Saul dead, David was the rightfully anointed king of Israel and should have been able to take the throne. But a man named Abner had other ideas:

2 Samuel 2:8 *But Abner the son of Ner, captain of Saul's host, took Ishbosheth the son of Saul, and brought him over to Mahanaim; 9 And made him king over Gilead, and over the Ashurites, and over Jezreel, and over Ephraim, and over Benjamin, and over all Israel. 10 Ishbosheth Saul's son was forty years old when he began to reign over Israel, and reigned two years. But the house of Judah followed David. 11 And the time that David was king in Hebron over the house of Judah was seven years and six months.*

The nation was now divided, with the tribe of Judah following David as king, and everyone else following Ishbosheth. And this arrangement lasted for seven and a half long years.

Did David have a right to rule the entire nation? Yes.

But did that "right" make it happen? No.

And many times, it is just like that in our lives. It is not always the "right" that makes things happen in our lives, but the patience to endure until that right becomes reality! Many people get so frustrated by not immediately getting the things that they have a right to that they throw up their hands in frustration and quit. But the people that focus on doing right rather than screaming about their rights endure and eventually prevail. So, DO focus more on doing right than on screaming about your rights!

Personal Notes:

_____
_____
_____
_____
_____
_____
_____
_____
_____
_____
_____
_____
_____
_____
_____
_____
_____
_____
_____
_____
_____
_____
_____
_____
_____
_____
_____
_____
_____

Devotion 04

Neither side was going to forever be content with a divided kingdom. And, as Ishbosheth and Abner, his general, controlled eleven of the twelve tribes, they felt like they could be the aggressors in the issue.

So, Abner and some of his men came to Gibeon, right by the border of Judah. Naturally, an enemy force this close to the border brought a response from David and his general, Joab.

2 Samuel 2:12 *And Abner the son of Ner, and the servants of Ishbosheth the son of Saul, went out from Mahanaim to Gibeon.* **13** *And Joab the son of Zeruiah, and the servants of David, went out, and met together by the pool of Gibeon: and they sat down, the one on the one side of the pool, and the other on the other side of the pool.*

Behold the uneasy stare-down; Joab's men on one side of the water, Abner's men just across from them on the other side. And it was then that Abner suggested that a small number of men go at it. And they did. But what an odd battle it was!

2 Samuel 2:15 *Then there arose and went over by number twelve of Benjamin, which pertained to Ishbosheth the son of Saul, and twelve of the servants of David.* **16** *And they caught every one his fellow by the head, and thrust his sword in his fellow's side; so they fell down together: wherefore that place was called Helkathhazzurim, which is in Gibeon.*

Apparently, this is what happens when everyone is reading the same "Big Book of Battle Tactics." Step one: wrap your left arm around your opponent's head. Step two: with your right hand, jab your sword into their side and kill them."

Does anyone notice the "missing element" here? If both hands are being used offensively, there is nothing at all left for defense! In other words, this is a great way to kill; it is also a great way to get killed. Twenty-four men fought, and all twenty-four died the exact same way.

If you do things the exact same way everyone else does them, you will get the exact same results everyone else gets. That being the case, there is something to be said for individuality! Doctrine is non-negotiable, and sin is always sin. But within the boundaries of what is right, remember that God made you utterly unique. There simply is not another "you" anywhere! So, DO be you!

Personal Notes:

_____

_____

_____

_____

_____

_____

_____

_____

_____

_____

_____

_____

_____

_____

_____

_____

Devotion 05

After the odd and fatal battle before the battle in which all twenty-four participants died, the greater battle resulted in a one-sided rout:

2 Samuel 2:17 *And there was a very sore battle that day; and Abner was beaten, and the men of Israel, before the servants of David.*

That rout sent General Abner and his men running for their lives. And that pursuit resulted in another death.

2 Samuel 2:18 *And there were three sons of Zeruiah there, Joab, and Abishai, and Asahel: and Asahel was as light of foot as a wild roe.* **19** *And Asahel pursued after Abner; and in going he turned not to the right hand nor to the left from following Abner.* **20** *Then Abner looked behind him, and said, Art thou Asahel? And he answered, I am.* **21** *And Abner said to him, Turn thee aside to thy right hand or to thy left, and lay thee hold on one of the young men, and take thee his armour. But Asahel would not turn aside from following of him.* **22** *And Abner said again to Asahel, Turn thee aside from following me: wherefore should I smite thee to the ground? how then should I hold up my face to Joab thy brother?* **23** *Howbeit he refused to turn aside: wherefore Abner with the hinder end of the spear smote him under the fifth rib, that the spear came out behind him; and he fell down there, and died in the same place: and it came to pass, that as many as came to the place where Asahel fell down and died stood still.*

We always think of war as an impersonal thing between people who do not know each other. But that is not always the case. Abner knew Asahel.

He also knew his brother, Joab, the General of the opposition. He did not want to kill him, but Asahel left him no choice, and so he did.

In any conflict, someone is going to get hurt or killed. That being the case, none of us should be quick to engage in conflict. If forced upon us, we should be brave enough to stand; but those who seek conflict or take conflict lightly do not understand how God expects us to feel about lives or hearts.

DO be compassionate enough toward others to not rush to conflict!

Personal Notes:

_____
_____
_____
_____
_____
_____
_____
_____
_____
_____
_____
_____
_____
_____
_____
_____
_____
_____
_____
_____
_____

Devotion 06

It had been Abner and his forces that were the aggressors in coming toward Judah's borders. It had been Abner that suggested that twelve of his men fight twelve of Joab's men, resulting in twenty-four deaths. But after that, when running from Asahel, he clearly began to think differently, and only killed the young man when left with no choice. And within just a few more hours we find him even less willing to continue the bloodshed:

2 Samuel 2:24 *Joab also and Abishai pursued after Abner: and the sun went down when they were come to the hill of Ammah, that lieth before Giah by the way of the wilderness of Gibeon. 25 And the children of Benjamin gathered themselves together after Abner, and became one troop, and stood on the top of an hill. 26 Then Abner called to Joab, and said, Shall the sword devour for ever? knowest thou not that it will be bitterness in the latter end? how long shall it be then, ere thou bid the people return from following their brethren? 27 And Joab said, As God liveth, unless thou hadst spoken, surely then in the morning the people had gone up every one from following his brother. 28 So Joab blew a trumpet, and all the people stood still, and pursued after Israel no more, neither fought they any more.*

Making a last stand on the top of a hill, Abner called for a truce. One day of battle had been enough to change his mind on its need or value. But one cannot help but wonder if his mind would have been thus changed had he not ended up on the losing side of things! Fortunately for him, for once, Joab showed some restraint. That is all the more remarkable considering the death of his brother at the hands of Abner.

This tendency to make decisions based on how it affects us is universal to man, but that does not make it right. DO make a habit of considering others when you make your decisions. If God Himself had not done so, there never would have been a Calvary!

Personal Notes:

_____

_____

_____

_____

_____

_____

_____

_____

_____

_____

_____

_____

_____

_____

_____

_____

_____

_____

_____

_____

_____

_____

_____

_____

Devotion 07

It was Abner that had placed Ishbosheth, the son of Saul, on the throne of Israel. But in 2 Samuel 3 Abner and Ishbosheth had a falling out, and it was so bad that Abner boldly declared that he would give the entire kingdom to David. And since he was the power behind the throne, and Ishbosheth just a weak figurehead, he had the ability to do so.

When Abner sent David word of his intentions, David sent back word with one non-negotiable requirement before there would be any league between them.

2 Samuel 3:13 *And he said, Well; I will make a league with thee: but one thing I require of thee, that is, Thou shalt not see my face, except thou first bring Michal Saul's daughter, when thou comest to see my face.* **14** *And David sent messengers to Ishbosheth Saul's son, saying, Deliver me my wife Michal, which I espoused to me for an hundred foreskins of the Philistines.* **15** *And Ishbosheth sent, and took her from her husband, even from Phaltiel the son of Laish.* **16** *And her husband went with her along weeping behind her to Bahurim. Then said Abner unto him, Go, return. And he returned.*

When David had been on the run from Saul for so very long, Saul, to spite David, did a horrible thing. He gave his daughter, David's wife, to another man. Michal lost David, then was with Phaltiel for a good long while, and was ripped away from him. We all remember Michal for her explosion at David a short time later in 2 Samuel 6, but before that happened she had her world thrown into a tailspin over and over again by the men in her life. Before she was an angry wife, she was an innocent victim of men and their power struggles.

No woman should ever be put in such a horrible position. Men, if God thinks enough of you to give you a wife, or a daughter, be as thoughtful of them as Christ Himself would be if He were in your place. DO understand that the Lord would never put His needs and desires above the needs and desires of the precious ladies in His life, nor should we!

Personal Notes:

_____

_____

_____

_____

_____

_____

_____

_____

_____

_____

_____

_____

_____

_____

_____

_____

_____

_____

_____

_____

_____

_____

Devotion 08

Having secured Michal for David, Abner came to him in Hebron and began the process of delivering the entire kingdom into his hand. Behaving in an honorable manner, David sent him away in peace.

But shortly thereafter General Joab showed back up. Joab, remember, had a personal grudge against Abner anyway since Abner killed his brother, Asahel. When Joab found out that Abner had been to see David, and that David had let him leave in peace, he went ballistic:

2 Samuel 3:24 *Then Joab came to the king, and said, What hast thou done? behold, Abner came unto thee; why is it that thou hast sent him away, and he is quite gone?* **25** *Thou knowest Abner the son of Ner, that he came to deceive thee, and to know thy going out and thy coming in, and to know all that thou doest.* **26** *And when Joab was come out from David, he sent messengers after Abner, which brought him again from the well of Sirah: but David knew it not.* **27** *And when Abner was returned to Hebron, Joab took him aside in the gate to speak with him quietly, and smote him there under the fifth rib, that he died, for the blood of Asahel his brother.*

Joab murdered Abner. This would be the first of a great many times that Joab defied the express wishes of David, his king. And it would one day culminate in Joab killing David's son, Absalom. Had David dealt with Joab here in this first instance, he could have likely prevented the murder of his son many years later.

DO deal with things that need to be dealt with rather than punting them down the road; things left for later have the one thing you do not need them to have -- time to get worse!

Personal Notes:

_____

_____

_____

_____

_____

_____

_____

_____

_____

_____

_____

_____

_____

_____

_____

_____

_____

_____

_____

_____

_____

_____

_____

_____

Devotion 09

As David reacted to the news that Joab had murdered Abner, he spoke words both of condemnation toward Joab and consternation toward Abner.

2 Samuel 3:33 *And the king lamented over Abner, and said, Died Abner as a fool dieth?* **34** *Thy hands were not bound, nor thy feet put into fetters: as a man falleth before wicked men, so fellest thou. And all the people wept again over him.* **35** *And when all the people came to cause David to eat meat while it was yet day, David sware, saying, So do God to me, and more also, if I taste bread, or ought else, till the sun be down.* **36** *And all the people took notice of it, and it pleased them: as whatsoever the king did pleased all the people.* **37** *For all the people and all Israel understood that day that it was not of the king to slay Abner the son of Ner.* **38** *And the king said unto his servants, Know ye not that there is a prince and a great man fallen this day in Israel?* **39** *And I am this day weak, though anointed king; and these men the sons of Zeruiah be too hard for me: the LORD shall reward the doer of evil according to his wickedness.*

In Joab's presence, David referred to him in terms of wickedness. But it is what he said of Abner that is so poignant. Yes, he called him a prince and a great man, but he also asked the question "died Abner as a fool dieth?" And yes, though he did not mean to, he did. To allow a man like Joab to get anywhere near him and not be on the defensive was foolish.

But how many people still die as fools today? They die as drunk fools, stoned fools, criminal fools, lonely fools due to behavior that pushed everyone away, unfaithful fools whose dead body is rolled into a church that their living body was not in for years, and even lost fools who rejected Christ and have an eternity to regret it.

If everyone knew the day of their death, it would be easy to not die as a fool. But since no one knows the day of their death, the only way not to die like a fool is to spend every day not living like a fool. DO refuse to live and die like a fool!

Personal Notes:

_____

_____

_____

_____

_____

_____

_____

_____

_____

_____

_____

_____

_____

_____

_____

_____

_____

_____

_____

_____

_____

Devotion 10

In 2 Samuel 4, Ishbosheth, the son of Saul, was murdered by two of his own men. Those men then came to David to tell him what they had done, seeking his favor. Does that sound familiar? Just a couple of chapters earlier an Amalekite tried the same thing, claiming to have killed Saul. And David reacted the same way this time as he did with that Amalekite:

2 Samuel 4:9 *And David answered Rechab and Baanah his brother, the sons of Rimmon the Beerothite, and said unto them, As the LORD liveth, who hath redeemed my soul out of all adversity,* **10** *When one told me, saying, Behold, Saul is dead, thinking to have brought good tidings, I took hold of him, and slew him in Ziklag, who thought that I would have given him a reward for his tidings:* **11** *How much more, when wicked men have slain a righteous person in his own house upon his bed? shall I not therefore now require his blood of your hand, and take you away from the earth?* **12** *And David commanded his young men, and they slew them, and cut off their hands and their feet, and hanged them up over the pool in Hebron. But they took the head of Ishbosheth, and buried it in the sepulchre of Abner in Hebron.*

This was a fairly consistent practice with David. Saul tried to destroy him over and over again, yet every time someone murdered (or claimed to have murdered) a member of the house of Saul, David took their life for it. He was showing reverence for the position of the king. And, since he would be the next king over all the land, that was one of the wisest patterns he could ever establish!

It is incredibly foolish to behave dishonorably toward people (pastors, officers, officials, parents, etc.) and then expect that not to come back on us like a boomerang once we are in a position of authority. If you expect others to one day behave honorably toward you and yours, DO right now behave honorably toward them and theirs!

Personal Notes:

_____

_____

_____

_____

_____

_____

_____

_____

_____

_____

_____

_____

_____

_____

_____

_____

_____

_____

_____

_____

_____

_____

Devotion 11

At long last, the battle between David and the house of Saul was over. And, seeing that they now had no king, no shepherd, all of the tribes came to David seeking to be unified under his reign.

2 Samuel 5:1 *Then came all the tribes of Israel to David unto Hebron, and spake, saying, Behold, we are thy bone and thy flesh.* **2** *Also in time past, when Saul was king over us, thou wast he that leddest out and broughtest in Israel: and the LORD said to thee, Thou shalt feed my people Israel, and thou shalt be a captain over Israel.* **3** *So all the elders of Israel came to the king to Hebron; and king David made a league with them in Hebron before the LORD: and they anointed David king over Israel.* **4** *David was thirty years old when he began to reign, and he reigned forty years.*

It is what these people said in verse two that is so very telling. When Saul was alive and on the throne, he held the position of King, but it was David who held their heart. It was David who made himself accessible to all of them and made himself a servant to everyone. And years later, based on the character that they had seen in him since the time he was just a child, everyone came to him and asked for his leadership.

Having a position is one thing; having the heart of the people is quite another. We will all be given various positions throughout our lives, but if we do not carefully cultivate a relationship with the people over whom we are servant leaders, we have nothing but an empty crown.

DO think more of the people than of any position you hold over people! Anyone can come up with a crown to wear; only true leaders win the heart of the people to such a degree that people seek them out for leadership.

Personal Notes:

_____

_____

_____

_____

_____

_____

_____

_____

_____

_____

_____

_____

_____

_____

_____

_____

_____

_____

_____

_____

_____

_____

_____

_____

_____

_____

_____

_____

Devotion 12

Now unquestionably established as king over all the people, David began the process of making progress in the kingdom. And the first order of business was to conquer a city that should have been in their control but was not.

2 Samuel 5:6 *And the king and his men went to Jerusalem unto the Jebusites, the inhabitants of the land: which spake unto David, saying, Except thou take away the blind and the lame, thou shalt not come in hither: thinking, David cannot come in hither.* **7** *Nevertheless David took the strong hold of Zion: the same is the city of David.* **8** *And David said on that day, Whosoever getteth up to the gutter, and smiteth the Jebusites, and the lame and the blind, that are hated of David's soul, he shall be chief and captain. Wherefore they said, The blind and the lame shall not come into the house.*

This is one of the oddest passages of Scripture in the entire Bible. And the entire point of this devotion is just how very odd it is!

When David and his men went to take Jerusalem, some people called the Jebusites held the city. When they saw David coming, they looked over the walls and started shouting an insult that went something like this; "our city is so great and so secure, and David and his men are so weak and pitiful, that we could let blind and lame people defend it, and David could not overcome it. Nyah Nyah Nyah, we're better than David."

In other words, when David spoke of hating the lame and the blind, it literally had nothing to do with actual lame and blind people. This was a battle of insults. And when we read Scripture, we must learn to study and figure out things like that lest we miss the entire point! Scripture is not a comic book to be entertained by or a newspaper to mindlessly scroll; it is the eternal Word of God and must be studied as such.

DO be much more than a casual reader of Scripture; be an avid student of Scripture!

Personal Notes:

_____

_____

_____

_____

_____

_____

_____

_____

_____

_____

_____

_____

_____

_____

_____

_____

_____

_____

_____

_____

_____

_____

Devotion 13

David conquered the city of Jerusalem and brought it into the fold of Israel. And then, as the colloquialism goes, he was off and running.

2 Samuel 5:9 *So David dwelt in the fort, and called it the city of David. And David built round about from Millo and inward.* **10** *And David went on, and grew great, and the LORD God of hosts was with him.* **11** *And Hiram king of Tyre sent messengers to David, and cedar trees, and carpenters, and masons: and they built David an house.* **12** *And David perceived that the LORD had established him king over Israel, and that he had exalted his kingdom for his people Israel's sake.*

David gained the victory at Jerusalem and named it the city of David. He had emissaries from a wealthy foreign king bringing great gifts and supplies and workers for him to build a house for himself.

Seeing this, David rightly concluded that the Lord had, in fact, established him as king over Israel. But much more importantly, David figured out why:

2 Samuel 5:12 *And David perceived that the LORD had established him king over Israel, and that he had exalted his kingdom for his people Israel's sake.*

God did not do all of this for David for David's sake; He did all of this for David for Israel's sake. We do well to remember each and every time God exalts us, that He is doing so for the purpose of our being a help and a blessing to others, not so that we may greedily hoard things to ourselves or lift ourselves up in pride.

DO reflect today on the fact that when God does something great for you, He has not done so just for you!

Personal Notes:

_____

_____

_____

_____

_____

_____

_____

_____

_____

_____

_____

_____

_____

_____

_____

_____

_____

_____

_____

_____

_____

_____

_____

_____

_____

_____

Devotion 14

For David, who had spent so many years on the run, and then so many more years as king over only one of the twelve tribes, things were finally going so very right. All the tribes were united under his hand, foreign kings were sending gifts and treasurers, it seemed that nothing could go wrong. And then...

2 Samuel 5:17 *But when the Philistines heard that they had anointed David king over Israel, all the Philistines came up to seek David; and David heard of it, and went down to the hold.*

When the Philistines came seeking David, this verse says that "all" of them came up. And they were not carrying streamers and party favors. This was an overwhelming attack force designed to destroy the new Kng of Israel. The Philistines knew the capability of David, and they knew how powerful Israel would surely become under his rule if he lived. So they came up seeking to cut off the head so that the body would die...

Do you have a pastor that leads well? Parents that stand for God and keep the family on the right track? An employer who does not hesitate to let his witness for Christ shine in the workplace? Some political leader who leads righteously in word and deed? DO intentionally bring to mind every day the fact that the devil desperately wants to destroy them. And then DO pray for them as if your prayers will be the deciding factor on whether or not he is able to do so!

Personal Notes:

_____

_____

_____

_____

_____

_____

_____

_____

_____

_____

_____

_____

_____

_____

_____

_____

_____

_____

_____

_____

_____

_____

_____

_____

_____

_____

_____

_____

Devotion 15

When David realized that the Philistines were coming after him, he did not sit back passively in a defensive posture and wait for them.

2 Samuel 5:18 *The Philistines also came and spread themselves in the valley of Rephaim.* **19** *And David enquired of the LORD, saying, Shall I go up to the Philistines? wilt thou deliver them into mine hand? And the LORD said unto David, Go up: for I will doubtless deliver the Philistines into thine hand.* **20** *And David came to Baalperazim, and David smote them there, and said, The LORD hath broken forth upon mine enemies before me, as the breach of waters. Therefore he called the name of that place Baalperazim.*

David and his men won a great victory over the Philistines that day. And because of that, they renamed that place Baalperazim. You surely recognize the name Baal in the first part of that word. The last half of that word means "breaches" or "breaks." In other words, this would now be known as "the place where Baal was broken." And the next verse bears that out even further:

2 Samuel 5:21 *And there they left their images, and David and his men burned them.*

The Philistines ran and left their pitiful little "gods" behind them. David and Israel, in sharp contrast to how Israel usually behaved during the time of the judges, burned those idols. In years gone by they would have been dumb enough to worship the very false gods that their God had just defeated!

When you look at the seeming power of the wickedness of this world, DO think back to Calvary and remember that the head of Satan was "bruised" (crushed and broken) there! It was his "Devilperazim." He still exists, he still roars and rages, but his doom was sealed by a cross and an empty tomb!

Personal Notes:

_____

_____

_____

_____

_____

_____

_____

_____

_____

_____

_____

_____

_____

_____

_____

_____

_____

_____

_____

_____

_____

_____

_____

_____

_____

_____

_____

_____

Devotion 16

David won a great head-to-head victory against the Philistines at Baalperazim, the valley of Rephaim. Shortly thereafter, though, they came back again. David, who could easily have assumed that he could and should do exactly what he did last time, instead did something much wiser. He checked with God first.

2 Samuel 5:23 *And when David enquired of the LORD, he said, Thou shalt not go up; but fetch a compass behind them, and come upon them over against the mulberry trees.* **24** *And let it be, when thou hearest the sound of a going in the tops of the mulberry trees, that then thou shalt bestir thyself: for then shall the LORD go out before thee, to smite the host of the Philistines.*

God gave David a completely different battle plan the second time around. David and his men were to circle around behind them, and then wait for God to signal them by the sound of "going in the mulberry trees." What exactly that sound was has been the subject of wide speculation. Some commentators view it as just the sound of the wind, and an Arabic text says that it was the sound of horses hooves in the trees! Whatever sound it was, David knew it meant that was the moment to come out of hiding and fight, because God would be going ahead of them to fight for them.

And He did, and they won.

Could God have given them the victory the second time the exact same way that He did the first? Certainly. But the victory was not the ultimate goal;

getting David and the people to seek God's guidance for everything was the goal.

Don't assume, and DO seek God's guidance in whatever you face today!

Personal Notes:

_____

_____

_____

_____

_____

_____

_____

_____

_____

_____

_____

_____

_____

_____

_____

_____

_____

_____

_____

_____

_____

_____

_____

_____

_____

Devotion 17

In 2 Samuel 6, King David turned his attention from war to a much more pressing matter. For somewhere in the neighborhood of fifty or sixty years, the ark of the covenant had been almost entirely a forgotten thing in the land. It had been lost during the days of Eli the priest, returned to the land, and only once called for during the entire forty-year reign of Saul. But David, the man after God's own heart, was determined to change all of that.

And so, accompanied by 30,000 men, David went to retrieve the ark. But unfortunately, especially for one man in particular, that is when things went horribly, spectacularly wrong.

2 Samuel 6:3 *And they set the ark of God upon a new cart, and brought it out of the house of Abinadab that was in Gibeah: and Uzzah and Ahio, the sons of Abinadab, drave the new cart.* **4** *And they brought it out of the house of Abinadab which was at Gibeah, accompanying the ark of God: and Ahio went before the ark.* **5** *And David and all the house of Israel played before the LORD on all manner of instruments made of fir wood, even on harps, and on psalteries, and on timbrels, and on cornets, and on cymbals.* **6** *And when they came to Nachon's threshingfloor, Uzzah put forth his hand to the ark of God, and took hold of it; for the oxen shook it.* **7** *And the anger of the LORD was kindled against Uzzah; and God smote him there for his error; and there he died by the ark of God.*

This man, Uzzah, was not someone who was unfamiliar with the ark of the covenant. In fact, he should have been more familiar with it than most anyone in the nation; he had grown up with it in his house! He, of all people, should have known never to touch it.

As great of a danger as being unfamiliar with God is, being too familiar with God is almost as great of a danger. When we lose the reverential fear and awe of God that we ought to have, disaster is not likely far away for an individual or a family or a church.

DO remember that the God who loves us and sent His Son to die for us is still also the God that we are to revere and fear!

Personal Notes:

_____

_____

_____

_____

_____

_____

_____

_____

_____

_____

_____

_____

_____

_____

_____

_____

_____

_____

_____

Devotion 18

After Uzzah's untimely death, David did not know what to do with the ark. So he simply carried it to a nearby house and left it there.

2 Samuel 6:9 *And David was afraid of the LORD that day, and said, How shall the ark of the LORD come to me?* **10** *So David would not remove the ark of the LORD unto him into the city of David: but David carried it aside into the house of Obededom the Gittite.*

I would imagine that, given the rather public death of Uzzah, Obededom was probably terrified at the thought of the ark of God being in his house. But it quickly became evident that it was the best thing that ever happened to the household:

2 Samuel 6:11 *And the ark of the LORD continued in the house of Obededom the Gittite three months: and the LORD blessed Obededom, and all his household.* **12** *And it was told king David, saying, The LORD hath blessed the house of Obededom, and all that pertaineth unto him, because of the ark of God. So David went and brought up the ark of God from the house of Obededom into the city of David with gladness.*

Not only was Obededom blessed because of the ark, all of his household was as well. Wife, kids, crops, livestock, everything was getting stronger, healthier, more prosperous. The blessings became so evident that word of them got back to David, who quickly then retrieved the ark and brought it into the city of David.

The presence of God made all the difference. And it still does.

DO refuse to settle for just "being saved." Cultivate a day by day close relationship with the God who saved you. Value His presence, and you will be blessed with His presents as well!

Personal Notes:

_____

_____

_____

_____

_____

_____

_____

_____

_____

_____

_____

_____

_____

_____

_____

_____

_____

_____

_____

_____

_____

_____

_____

_____

_____

_____

_____

Devotion 19

Bringing the ark of God into the city and getting it set up in the tabernacle that he pitched for it was one of the greatest days in David's life and in Israel's history. There was a nationwide celebration. But one person out of that nation was not in a celebrating mood, not at all.

2 Samuel 6:18 *And as soon as David had made an end of offering burnt offerings and peace offerings, he blessed the people in the name of the LORD of hosts.* **19** *And he dealt among all the people, even among the whole multitude of Israel, as well to the women as men, to every one a cake of bread, and a good piece of flesh, and a flagon of wine. So all the people departed every one to his house.* **20** *Then David returned to bless his household. And Michal the daughter of Saul came out to meet David, and said, How glorious was the king of Israel to day, who uncovered himself to day in the eyes of the handmaids of his servants, as one of the vain fellows shamelessly uncovereth himself!*

Michal erupted at David and was both unjustified in doing so and incorrect in what she assumed. She accused him of being uncovered (naked) but verse fourteen says that he was wearing a linen ephod.

Wrong? Yes. But David's response was no better:

2 Samuel 6:21 *And David said unto Michal, It was before the LORD, which chose me before thy father, and before all his house, to appoint me ruler over the people of the LORD, over Israel: therefore will I play before the LORD.* **22** *And I will yet be more* *vile than thus, and will be base in mine own sight: and of the maidservants which thou hast spoken of, of them shall I be had in honour.* **23** *Therefore Michal the daughter of Saul had no child unto the day of her death.*

David escalated what Michal started, and the end result of what they both did was a ruined marriage, a marriage that had started as a true love story.

DO remember that God gave husbands and wives each other to be treated as lovingly and carefully as He treats us. Before you ruin a home, take a breath, take a few steps back, and ask yourself, "Is what I am about to do and say the same thing that the Lord would do or say in my place?" If it isn't, DO and say something else!

Personal Notes:

_____

_____

_____

_____

_____

_____

_____

_____

_____

_____

_____

_____

_____

_____

_____

Devotion 20

Many years earlier God had informed Samuel that he was going to seek a man after his own heart to be king. And the first two verses of 2 Samuel 7 show us how well God did at finding that very kind of a man.

2 Samuel 7:1 *And it came to pass, when the king sat in his house, and the LORD had given him rest round about from all his enemies;* **2** *That the king said unto Nathan the prophet, See now, I dwell in an house of cedar, but the ark of God dwelleth within curtains.*

Thanks to the help and generosity of men like Hiram, David's house was comfortable and elaborate. One day as David was sitting in his house, he began to think about the ark of God residing in just a simple tent. And something about that bothered David. So he called Nathan the prophet and pointed this out.

For David to even give this a second thought made him radically different than King Saul, who for forty years barely ever even had God or the ark cross his mind. That the ark of God should perhaps be housed in something much nicer would never have occurred to Saul, but it did occur to David, the man after God's own heart.

The "house of God" will be important to people who are after God's own heart. They will value it, they will expend time and treasure to make it something nice, and they will attend it. But unless one's heart is after God's own heart, that kind of thing will likely not make much sense.

Both Saul and David gave lip service to God, but only David showed true devotion to God by focusing attention on the house of God. DO be a David rather than a Saul!

Personal Notes:

_____

_____

_____

_____

_____

_____

_____

_____

_____

_____

_____

_____

_____

_____

_____

_____

_____

_____

_____

_____

_____

_____

_____

_____

_____

_____

_____

_____

Devotion 21

David wanted to build God a wonderful house. His desire was a good desire, and because of that Nathan the prophet assumed that it would be God's will. But later that night God spoke to Nathan and told him to go back to David with a different message. God did want a house built, but it would be David's son, Solomon, that would build the house, rather than David.

But why would it have to be that way, seeing that David was a man after God's own heart?

David had, by necessity, been a man of war and shed much blood, and that was the reason Solomon would be tasked with building the house instead of him:

1 Chronicles 28:3 *But God said unto me, Thou shalt not build an house for my name, because thou hast been a man of war, and hast shed blood.*

In other words, because David fought the battles, Solomon could enjoy the peace. There is a lesson in that, don't you think? Christian parents, especially, are tempted just to give in on everything, don't rock the boat, keep the kids and everyone else happy. But if our kids are to truly ever be able to experience a peaceful walk with God, it will likely only happen because godly parents had enough character to fight the battles for years before that.

DO be willing to fight those battles!

Personal Notes:

_____

_____

_____

_____

_____

_____

_____

_____

_____

_____

_____

_____

_____

_____

_____

_____

_____

_____

_____

_____

_____

_____

_____

_____

_____

_____

_____

_____

Devotion 22

All of 2 Samuel 8 deals with the battles and wars that David and Israel fought. Under the reign of Saul there had been battles, but very little success at winning those battles and turning them into larger successes for the entire kingdom. Under David, though, there were victories over the Philistines, Moab, Syria, Ammon, Amalek, Edom, and many more. This chapter lists much of the national wealth that was accumulated through these victories.

But there is a phrase repeated twice in this chapter that is the key to the entire list of victories gained:

2 Samuel 8:6 *Then David put garrisons in Syria of Damascus: and the Syrians became servants to David, and brought gifts. And the LORD preserved David whithersoever he went.*

2 Samuel 8:14 *And he put garrisons in Edom; throughout all Edom put he garrisons, and all they of Edom became David's servants. And the LORD preserved David whithersoever he went.*

"The LORD preserved David whithersoever he went." The fact that this phrase is repeated twice in near proximity lets us know that God wanted to emphasize it. David was a brave, skilled, tremendous fighter and a great organizer. But his success ultimately came from the fact that the Lord preserved him wherever he went.

Sometimes we tend to forget that even at our strongest, we can still be beaten, we can still lose, we can still fall. What each of us desperately needs is God preserving us!

When you pray, it is entirely appropriate to thank God for whatever strength and ability He has given you. But DO remember to pray for his preservation as well; without that, there is not a single moment that we are not at risk!

Personal Notes:

_____

_____

_____

_____

_____

_____

_____

_____

_____

_____

_____

_____

_____

_____

_____

_____

_____

_____

_____

_____

_____

_____

_____

_____

_____

Devotion 23

2 Samuel 9 contains one of the most precious accounts in Scripture, the account of David and Mephibosheth. From the very first verse of this account, there is such a wealth to learn about the way things ought to be.

2 Samuel 9:1 *And David said, Is there yet any that is left of the house of Saul, that I may shew him kindness for Jonathan's sake?*

To say that "the house of Saul" had been miserably cruel to David would be an understatement. It was because of the house of Saul that David spent much of his youth on the run for his life, sleeping outdoors, separated from those who loved him. It was because of the house of Saul that David, for seven long years, was only able to be king over a small part of the land instead of all of it.

And yet, one part of the house of Saul had been precious beyond price to David. The friendship of David and Jonathan, the son of Saul, was a true friendship, and Jonathan a true friend. And so, despite the commonly accepted practice in the ancient world of wiping out the entire family of the former, rival king, David instead went looking for any member of that family that he could show kindness to.

Things like this show us just how much a "man after God's own heart" David really was. It is ridiculous to claim to be a man or woman after God's own heart, and yet be petty and vindictive rather than show the type of graciousness and kindness that David showed here.

DO take stock of your own heart. Repent of and release any traces of pettiness and vindictiveness and allow God to fill that void with the graciousness and kindness that He would show if He were in your place!

Personal Notes:

_____
_____
_____
_____
_____
_____
_____
_____
_____
_____
_____
_____
_____
_____
_____
_____
_____
_____
_____
_____
_____
_____
_____
_____
_____

Devotion 24

David had asked whether or not there were any living members of the family of Saul. He quickly had an answer, and based on that answer, he sprang into action.

2 Samuel 9:2 *And there was of the house of Saul a servant whose name was Ziba. And when they had called him unto David, the king said unto him, Art thou Ziba? And he said, Thy servant is he.* **3** *And the king said, Is there not yet any of the house of Saul, that I may shew the kindness of God unto him? And Ziba said unto the king, Jonathan hath yet a son, which is lame on his feet.* **4** *And the king said unto him, Where is he? And Ziba said unto the king, Behold, he is in the house of Machir, the son of Ammiel, in Lodebar.* **5** *Then king David sent, and fetched him out of the house of Machir, the son of Ammiel, from Lodebar.* **6** *Now when Mephibosheth, the son of Jonathan, the son of Saul, was come unto David, he fell on his face, and did reverence. And David said, Mephibosheth. And he answered, Behold thy servant!* **7** *And David said unto him, Fear not: for I will surely shew thee kindness for Jonathan thy father's sake, and will restore thee all the land of Saul thy father; and thou shalt eat bread at my table continually.*

When David learned that Jonathan, his dearest friend, had a son, the fact that the son was lame was irrelevant to him. He sent for Mephibosheth, who doubtless thought he was about to be put to death. Little wonder then, that after calling him by name, the next words out of David's mouth were "fear not."

The king did not go after the pauper to kill him; he went after him to make him part of his own family. That sounds a whole lot like what God did for us, doesn't it...

Whenever the devil tells you that you are worthless, DO remember that the King of Glory knows you by name and came looking for you to make you part of His family!

Personal Notes:

_____

_____

_____

_____

_____

_____

_____

_____

_____

_____

_____

_____

_____

_____

_____

_____

_____

_____

_____

_____

_____

_____

Devotion 25

David did not just promise Mephibosheth that he would take care of him, he more than followed through on that promise:

2 Samuel 9:11b... *As for Mephibosheth, said the king, he shall eat at my table, as one of the king's sons.* **12** *And Mephibosheth had a young son, whose name was Micha. And all that dwelt in the house of Ziba were servants unto Mephibosheth.* **13** *So Mephibosheth dwelt in Jerusalem: for he did eat continually at the king's table; and was lame on both his feet.*

For David to find that Jonathan had a son must have been thrilling; to find out that he even had a grandson, unspeakably glorious. Mephibosheth, with nothing to offer, nonetheless, was seated at the king's table as if one of the king's own sons. This had everything to do with Jonathan and David's friendship and David's character in honoring the promises he made to that friend when they were both young and had far to go in life. As Jonathan died at the hand of the Philistines, one fear he never had to have was that David would break his word and kill his son.

How many people are that conscientious in honoring promises?

And yet everyone should be, especially Christians. Everyone should be able to automatically assume that if a Christian makes a promise, that promise will be fulfilled.

DO be so godly, so conscientious, so filled with integrity that if you give your word on something, people can live and die in the full assurance that you will honor your word!

Personal Notes:

_____

_____

_____

_____

_____

_____

_____

_____

_____

_____

_____

_____

_____

_____

_____

_____

_____

_____

_____

_____

_____

_____

_____

_____

_____

_____

_____

_____

Devotion 26

David was on a roll concerning kindness. He had Mephibosheth at his table and also Mephibosheth's son. As 2 Samuel 10 begins, he is still looking for people to show kindness to. And he did.

2 Samuel 10:1 *And it came to pass after this, that the king of the children of Ammon died, and Hanun his son reigned in his stead.* **2** *Then said David, I will shew kindness unto Hanun the son of Nahash, as his father shewed kindness unto me. And David sent to comfort him by the hand of his servants for his father. And David's servants came into the land of the children of Ammon.*

We do not know what kindness Nahash, this foreign king, had shown to David. Whatever it was, David wanted to return that kindness to Nahash's son upon Nahash's death. That is wonderful! But wait, there's more, and it isn't good:

2 Samuel 10:3 *And the princes of the children of Ammon said unto Hanun their lord, Thinkest thou that David doth honour thy father, that he hath sent comforters unto thee? hath not David rather sent his servants unto thee, to search the city, and to spy it out, and to overthrow it?* **4** *Wherefore Hanun took David's servants, and shaved off the one half of their beards, and cut off their garments in the middle, even to their buttocks, and sent them away.*

These princes, and the new king, Hanun, were as dumb as a bag of hair, and we will cover that in the next devotion. But for now just notice that David did something kind, and that kindness was repaid with horrible unkindness. When that happens, what is the natural reaction concerning doing future kindnesses to others? We instinctively want to pull back and just "take care of me and mine."

But who gets the greatest joy from kindness? Consistently, the one doing the kindness! DO continue to be kind, even when it "goes bad;" whoever repays kindness with unkindness will suffer the consequences, making others unlikely to be kind to them. But since you get the greatest joy from being kind, DO continue to be kind!

Personal Notes:

_____
_____
_____
_____
_____
_____
_____
_____
_____
_____
_____
_____
_____
_____
_____
_____
_____
_____
_____
_____

Devotion 27

The messengers of David were treated incredibly rudely by Hanun and his men. One-half of their beards were shaved off of every man, and the backside of their garments was cut off right up to their buttocks. This was humiliation of the worst nature. In the next devotion, we will see how David took action against the perpetrators. But before we get to that, notice something else very important to learn from this.

2 Samuel 10:5 *When they told it unto David, he sent to meet them, because the men were greatly ashamed: and the king said, Tarry at Jericho until your beards be grown, and then return.*

The men who had their beards cut off and their buttocks left shining for the world to see were ashamed... at the loss of their beards. We would think that the memory of the buttock baring would be that which bothered them the most, but the loss of the beards bothered them far more, and not simply because it took longer to get that back. You see, grown men in that culture were expected to look like and act like men, and for them, that included having full beards.

Our culture does not look at beards on men in quite the same way, nor does Scripture mandate it (or condemn it), but the principle of men being manly in appearance and actions is still the same. Men should look like men. Men should act like men. The only "toxic masculinity" is effemininity!

Men, DO be manly!

Personal Notes:

Devotion 28

David's men, humiliated by the Ammonites, were hiding out at Jericho. David had sent them to Hanun out of kindness, since Hanun's father had died, wanting to comfort him.

Hanun, listening to the very poor counsel of his men, took those messengers, cut off the back of their clothes thus baring their buttocks, and shaved off half of their beards.

Not surprisingly, David was not happy.

2 Samuel 10:6 *And when the children of Ammon saw that they stank before David, the children of Ammon sent and hired the Syrians of Beth-rehob, and the Syrians of Zoba, twenty thousand footmen, and of king Maacah a thousand men, and of Ish-tob twelve thousand men.*

They saw that they "stank" before David. To quote the younger crowd today, "Ya think?"

Not much can make a person stink worse than repaying kindness with cruelty. And yet how often do we either do that very thing or at least respond to kindness with apathy or forgetfulness?

DO recognize and remember the kindnesses done to you along the way. Nothing makes kindness more likely to evaporate than acting like those kindnesses never even happened!

Personal Notes:

_____
_____
_____
_____
_____
_____
_____
_____
_____
_____
_____
_____
_____
_____
_____
_____
_____
_____
_____
_____
_____
_____
_____
_____
_____
_____
_____
_____
_____

Devotion 29

Realizing that David and his army were going to be marching against them for what they had done, the Ammonites quickly hired some help to defend themselves.

2 Samuel 10:6 *And when the children of Ammon saw that they stank before David, the children of Ammon sent and hired the Syrians of Bethrehob, and the Syrians of Zoba, twenty thousand footmen, and of king Maacah a thousand men, and of Ishtob twelve thousand men.*

Thirty-four thousand men. That, along with the warriors of the Ammonites, was a formidable force. When General Joab of David's army realized what he was facing, here is what he did.

2 Samuel 10:9 *When Joab saw that the front of the battle was against him before and behind, he chose of all the choice men of Israel, and put them in array against the Syrians:* **10** *And the rest of the people he delivered into the hand of Abishai his brother, that he might put them in array against the children of Ammon.* **11** *And he said, If the Syrians be too strong for me, then thou shalt help me: but if the children of Ammon be too strong for thee, then I will come and help thee.*

Joab realized that this was a situation where he may either need help or need to give help. He committed to doing whichever of those things was necessary.

And if I ask you which of those two things is hardest for you, most everyone will come up with the same answer...

Not many of us have trouble giving help when it is needed. But something about the pride in us makes it very difficult for us to ask for or receive help when we are the ones in need. But Joab, for all his faults, was a man willing to take help if needed.

DO be willing either to give or to receive help as the situation may demand; if you live long enough, you will find yourself on different sides of that line on a great many occasions!

Personal Notes:

_____

_____

_____

_____

_____

_____

_____

_____

_____

_____

_____

_____

_____

_____

_____

_____

_____

_____

_____

_____

_____

Devotion 30

2 Kings 10 ended with an overwhelming victory for the forces of Israel. But as chapter eleven begins, we find another large battle taking shape, but we also find a much more subtle battle in the making.

2 Samuel 11:1 *And it came to pass, after the year was expired, at the time when kings go forth to battle, that David sent Joab, and his servants with him, and all Israel; and they destroyed the children of Ammon, and besieged Rabbah. But David tarried still at Jerusalem. 2 And it came to pass in an eveningtide, that David arose from off his bed, and walked upon the roof of the king's house: and from the roof he saw a woman washing herself; and the woman was very beautiful to look upon.*

In the battle at end of chapter 10, the Syrians had taken the brunt of the defeat. But the Ammonites, those who had so insulted David's ambassadors, had still not been properly dealt with. So in the spring of the following year, the time when kings would once again take their armies into the field for battle, David sent the army after the Ammonites again. They made such good progress that they found themselves besieging the capital city of Rabbah. Not much could have been more important at that moment;

But David tarried still at Jerusalem.

That is not where he should have been. And that one small mistake was going to lead to the greatest downfall of his entire life. Seeing him residing comfortably and lazily in Jerusalem, the devil provided just the right temptation at just the right moment. We will say much about that in the next several devotions, but just for now understand that if

David had been where he was supposed to be, his great sin and downfall would have never happened.

People are always looking for the "secret" of doing right. It really isn't much of a secret at all; DO always be where you should be, and DO NOT ever be where you shouldn't be!

Personal Notes:

_____

_____

_____

_____

_____

_____

_____

_____

_____

_____

_____

_____

_____

_____

_____

_____

_____

_____

_____

_____

_____

_____

_____

_____

Devotion 31

While traveling down the highway of sin towards the destination of destruction, anyone paying even the remotest attention will see a great many warning billboards along the way, begging them to turn around. This was the case in David's great sin with Bathsheba.

2 Samuel 11:3 *And David sent and enquired after the woman. And one said, Is not this Bathsheba, the daughter of Eliam, the wife of Uriah the Hittite?*

When David asked who the woman was, warning signs began to slam him in the face one after the other. She was "the wife of..." and that should have been enough, no matter what name came next. There is literally no acceptable excuse anywhere ever for adultery. But another warning sign was the name of Eliam, her father. This was one of David's mighty men, his choicest and most loyal soldiers. Bathsheba was his daughter. And that provided another warning sign that was very visible to David, though not specified here in the verse. Eliam's father was named Ahithophel. Ahithophel, Bathsheba's grandfather, was David's most trusted counselor.

The last warning sign was that she was the wife of Uriah the Hittite, another one of David's mighty men, his choicest and most loyal soldiers. In other words, if David had said, "Who is the absolute, unquestioned, worst possible choice in the entire universe for me to have an affair with?" the name Bathsheba would have been on the very top of that list.

If you do wrong, DO understand that there will be no excuse for it; God always provides ample warning signs in His Word and in other ways to let us know we are going the wrong direction!

Personal Notes:

_____

_____

_____

_____

_____

_____

_____

_____

_____

_____

_____

_____

_____

_____

_____

_____

_____

_____

_____

_____

_____

_____

_____

_____

_____

_____

_____

_____

_____

Devotion 32

As the old saying goes, "Oh, what a tangled web we weave..."

2 Samuel 11:4 *And David sent messengers, and took her; and she came in unto him, and he lay with her; for she was purified from her uncleanness: and she returned unto her house.* **5** *And the woman conceived, and sent and told David, and said, I am with child.* **6** *And David sent to Joab, saying, Send me Uriah the Hittite. And Joab sent Uriah to David.* **7** *And when Uriah was come unto him, David demanded of him how Joab did, and how the people did, and how the war prospered.* **8** *And David said to Uriah, Go down to thy house, and wash thy feet. And Uriah departed out of the king's house, and there followed him a mess of meat from the king.*

While Uriah, one of David's best friends in the world, was away at war fighting on his behalf, David slept with his wife. What a horrible, unthinkable thing to do! No doubt he thought he had gotten by with it. And then came a message from Bathsheba; "I'm pregnant."

Suddenly David, who had, in his mind, gotten "too big for God to do without," found his world crashing down around him. And so he put what he believed was a foolproof plan in place to cover his sin. He called Uriah home from the field, made small talk, and then "sent Uriah home." His plan was obvious: get Uriah to sleep with his wife so that he would think the baby was his.

But do you realize what that would mean for David? If the plan succeeded, someone else would raise his child next door to him, with David never able to be a father to that precious child.

DO understand that the only truly good option concerning sin is never to sin to begin with! Once the deed is done, other than repentance, people find themselves left with only bad options.

Personal Notes:

_____

_____

_____

_____

_____

_____

_____

_____

_____

_____

_____

_____

_____

_____

_____

_____

_____

_____

_____

_____

_____

_____

_____

_____

Devotion 33

David tried multiple times to get Uriah to go spend the night with his wife, Bathsheba. But Uriah had too much character for that. He knew that it would not be proper for him to spend a night of pleasure with his wife while his compatriots were out in the field. And, seeing as how the army was right then at that moment besieging the very capital city of the enemy, everyone would need to be completely focused on the task, including him when he got back.

David realized he was beaten in this attempt at a cover-up. Would he confess what he had done? Would he take the punishment he so richly deserved? Sadly, no.

2 Samuel 11:14 *And it came to pass in the morning, that David wrote a letter to Joab, and sent it by the hand of Uriah.* **15** *And he wrote in the letter, saying, Set ye Uriah in the forefront of the hottest battle, and retire ye from him, that he may be smitten, and die.*

David determined to add murder to adultery. The man after God's own heart had cast all of that aside and was dancing with the devil cheek to cheek. But what I find fascinating at this point is that when he needed to commit the most horrendous of sins, he knew exactly who to go to to get the job done; Joab. He had previously verbally ripped Joab to shreds for Joab's murder of Abner; now he is enlisting Joab's help to murder Uriah.

What he did not grasp was that doing so would give Joab leverage over him for the rest of his life, leverage that eventually ended with Joab murdering David's pampered son, Absalom.

DO understand that there are no "your monsters;" there are just monsters. The monster that you nourish today, hoping to train it to eat others tomorrow, will eventually eat you.

Personal Notes:

_____

_____

_____

_____

_____

_____

_____

_____

_____

_____

_____

_____

_____

_____

_____

_____

_____

_____

_____

_____

_____

_____

_____

_____

_____

_____

Devotion 34

David's plan to murder Uriah worked perfectly, and a great man went to his death. For a few moments of pleasure, David murdered a friend. And while he may possibly have breathed a sigh of relief over his evil plan working, nothing good was coming from it.

2 Samuel 11:26 *And when the wife of Uriah heard that Uriah her husband was dead, she mourned for her husband.* **27** *And when the mourning was past, David sent and fetched her to his house, and she became his wife, and bare him a son. But the thing that David had done displeased the LORD.*

People through the years have endlessly speculated on how complicit Bathsheba was in all of this. One clue can be found in the words mourned in verse twenty-six, and mourning in verse twenty-seven. While mourning comes from a word that indicates the ritual of mourning, mourned comes from a completely different word and means to wail and to lament. Bathsheba lost a truly great man and showed utter brokenness over it.

But she was not the only one upset; verse twenty-seven tells us that the LORD Himself was also displeased.

And what of David? One of his dearest friends was dead, and his walk with the Lord was gone. Absolutely nobody won in any of this.

Before you choose to do wrong, realize that a sin will beget a coverup, a coverup will beget a bigger sin, and before you know it a few moments of pleasure will morph into a lifetime of agony all the way around.

DO right!

Personal Notes:

_____
_____
_____
_____
_____
_____
_____
_____
_____
_____
_____
_____
_____
_____
_____
_____
_____
_____
_____
_____
_____
_____
_____
_____
_____
_____
_____
_____
_____

Devotion 35

God was never going to let David get by with what he had done. And, in order to have that confrontation, God sent a man of God to him, a man named Nathan.

2 Samuel 12:1 *And the LORD sent Nathan unto David. And he came unto him, and said unto him, There were two men in one city; the one rich, and the other poor.* **2** *The rich man had exceeding many flocks and herds:* **3** *But the poor man had nothing, save one little ewe lamb, which he had bought and nourished up: and it grew up together with him, and with his children; it did eat of his own meat, and drank of his own cup, and lay in his bosom, and was unto him as a daughter.* **4** *And there came a traveller unto the rich man, and he spared to take of his own flock and of his own herd, to dress for the wayfaring man that was come unto him; but took the poor man's lamb, and dressed it for the man that was come to him.* **5** *And David's anger was greatly kindled against the man; and he said to Nathan, As the LORD liveth, the man that hath done this thing shall surely die:* **6** *And he shall restore the lamb fourfold, because he did this thing, and because he had no pity.* **7** *And Nathan said to David, Thou art the man...*

Two things leap out at me from these verses. One, David was so angry at this (imaginary) sinner that he was willing to put him to death, and for something far less serious than what he had done. People are often far harder on the minor sins of others than they are on their own heinous sins and those of their family. Two, Nathan, knowing that David had already murdered one man, nevertheless had the boldness and bravery to stand before him, stick his finger in his face, and say, "Thou art the man."

Thank God for a man of God willing to take such a risk! Most today would assuredly not do so, choosing instead to smile and speak of "grace." If you have a real man of God, DO thank God for him; he is a rarity in the modern world.

Personal Notes:

_____

_____

_____

_____

_____

_____

_____

_____

_____

_____

_____

_____

_____

_____

_____

_____

_____

_____

_____

_____

_____

_____

_____

_____

Devotion 36

As Nathan laid out for David the consequences of his sin, the severity of those consequences quickly became clear.

2 Samuel 12:7 *And Nathan said to David, Thou art the man. Thus saith the LORD God of Israel, I anointed thee king over Israel, and I delivered thee out of the hand of Saul;* **8** *And I gave thee thy master's house, and thy master's wives into thy bosom, and gave thee the house of Israel and of Judah; and if that had been too little, I would moreover have given unto thee such and such things.* **9** *Wherefore hast thou despised the commandment of the LORD, to do evil in his sight? thou hast killed Uriah the Hittite with the sword, and hast taken his wife to be thy wife, and hast slain him with the sword of the children of Ammon.* **10** *Now therefore the sword shall never depart from thine house; because thou hast despised me, and hast taken the wife of Uriah the Hittite to be thy wife.* **11** *Thus saith the LORD, Behold, I will raise up evil against thee out of thine own house, and I will take thy wives before thine eyes, and give them unto thy neighbour, and he shall lie with thy wives in the sight of this sun.* **12** *For thou didst it secretly: but I will do this thing before all Israel, and before the sun.*

What David did was not just going to land on him; his entire household would end up paying the price for it. This was part judgment and part prophecy. You see, it is not that God "stirred up trouble in his house" where there would never be any, as the text of Scripture unfolds we find David's sons simply following in his now evil footsteps. Would he repent?

Yes. But what he did would become known by all, including his own sons.

Our children learn from us, for good or bad. DO make every lesson they ever learn from your behavior and your words a good lesson!

Personal Notes:

_____

_____

_____

_____

_____

_____

_____

_____

_____

_____

_____

_____

_____

_____

_____

_____

_____

_____

_____

_____

_____

_____

_____

_____

Devotion 37

For David, despite all of the horrors of the punishments to come that Nathan the prophet had listed, the worst was still yet to come.

2 Samuel 12:13 *And David said unto Nathan, I have sinned against the LORD. And Nathan said unto David, The LORD also hath put away thy sin; thou shalt not die.* **14** *Howbeit, because by this deed thou hast given great occasion to the enemies of the LORD to blaspheme, the child also that is born unto thee shall surely die.* **15** *And Nathan departed unto his house. And the LORD struck the child that Uriah's wife bare unto David, and it was very sick.* **16** *David therefore besought God for the child; and David fasted, and went in, and lay all night upon the earth.* **17** *And the elders of his house arose, and went to him, to raise him up from the earth: but he would not, neither did he eat bread with them.* **18** *And it came to pass on the seventh day, that the child died...*

Do you notice how very desperate David was to save the life of his son and keep that child with him? At this moment in time, there was nothing more important to him. But do you remember what David's plan was when he was trying to cover up his sin with Bathsheba? David tried to get Uriah to sleep with his wife so that he would think the child was his, which would have resulted in David losing that child. But now, the very child that he was so quick to try and get rid of is the child that he is desperate to try and keep.

And he was not able to do so.

As the old saying goes, "You never know what you've got until it is gone." Many people have seemed quite anxious to give up marriages, parent-child relationships, friendships, and testimonies until those things were actually gone.

DO take stock of the treasures in your life, those things that you will have to give up for the pleasures of sin. And then DO fully realize that those treasures are worth far more than the sin that will take them from you!

Personal Notes:

_____

_____

_____

_____

_____

_____

_____

_____

_____

_____

_____

_____

_____

_____

_____

_____

_____

_____

_____

_____

_____

_____

_____

_____

Devotion 38

David had sinned the great sin that would stain his name for the rest of human history. His baby was now dead as a result of that sin. He was married to a woman whom he had stolen from another, having murdered her husband to do so. This account has, thus far, been all bad and all bleak. But oh, what a gracious and merciful God we serve!

2 Samuel 12:24 *And David comforted Bathsheba his wife, and went in unto her, and lay with her: and she bare a son, and he called his name Solomon: and the LORD loved him.* **25** *And he sent by the hand of Nathan the prophet; and he called his name Jedidiah, because of the LORD.*

If any of us were God (a truly horrifying thought!) I suspect David and Bathsheba would not have survived as a married couple, nor would God have allowed them to have any further children. But God allowed this marriage, which started as horrendously as possible, not only to survive but to thrive. God allowed this couple to have another son. And not only did God allow them that son, God Himself deeply love that son. God's name for Solomon was Jedidiah, meaning "beloved of Jehovah."

"How could God be so merciful and gracious in the face of such sinfulness! That just isn't right!" screams our flesh.

But the truth is, mercy and grace only seem "wrong" to us when it is extended to others. When it is extended to us, no matter how little we deserve it, we rejoice in it! But mercy and grace are only truly

"God-sized" when the righteous God of heaven extends it to those who are utterly unworthy.

And it is good that He does so since we are so very often utterly unworthy.

DO rejoice in the mercy and grace of God, whether extended to us or to others just as bad or worse than ourselves!

Personal Notes:

_____

_____

_____

_____

_____

_____

_____

_____

_____

_____

_____

_____

_____

_____

_____

_____

_____

_____

_____

_____

_____

_____

Devotion 39

The sin of David was behind him, but the prophesied fallout was just beginning.

2 Samuel 13:1 *And it came to pass after this, that Absalom the son of David had a fair sister, whose name was Tamar; and Amnon the son of David loved her.* **2** *And Amnon was so vexed, that he fell sick for his sister Tamar; for she was a virgin; and Amnon thought it hard for him to do any thing to her.* **3** *But Amnon had a friend, whose name was Jonadab, the son of Shimeah David's brother: and Jonadab was a very subtil man.* **4** *And he said unto him, Why art thou, being the king's son, lean from day to day? wilt thou not tell me? And Amnon said unto him, I love Tamar, my brother Absalom's sister.*

This was a sick, twisted, perverted desire on the part of Amnon. And anyone in the world with so much as an ounce of godliness would have told him so with no hesitation. Unfortunately, though, Amnon's "friend," Jonadab, was not burdened with even one of those ounces. In fact, Jonadab not only did not discourage Amnon from his wicked desire, he made it clear that, in his view, no desire on the part of Amnon should ever go unmet. He said, "Why art thou, being the king's son, lean from day to day?"

In other words, "Don't you know who you are? Come on, man, whatever you want, just take it!"

This entitlement mentality has affected our entire world these days, as shown by people marching through the streets demanding that every perverted desire of their hearts be met, subsidized, and even celebrated.

If only Amnon had a better friend. A real friend would have given him the counsel that hurt his feelings but saved his life.

DO cultivate real friends like that, and DO be such a real friend!

Personal Notes:

_____

_____

_____

_____

_____

_____

_____

_____

_____

_____

_____

_____

_____

_____

_____

_____

_____

_____

_____

_____

_____

_____

_____

_____

_____

_____

Devotion 40

After Jonadab gave Amnon the wicked plan for how to fulfill his twisted desires, Amnon raped his half-sister, Tamar. Then, seeing that she did not "respond joyfully" to what happened, he threw her out into the street.

And that is when her full brother, Absalom, found out what had happened. Absalom, for his part, told her to keep quiet about it. Tamar ended up living in shame in Absalom's home, unwanted by other men. Every bit of this was so very wicked that it deserved a forceful, thorough response from the king, who just so happened to be David, the father of everyone involved.

And what was David's response?

2 Samuel 13:21 *But when king David heard of all these things, he was very wroth.*

That is it. He was very angry. No punishment for anyone, no indication that anyone even got fussed at. He was just "angry." Why such a passive response from David when his own innocent daughter had been so violated, and her brother was so callous as to tell her to "keep quiet and forget about it?" That is easy to figure out; just say the names Bathsheba and Uriah...

David was afraid to say or do anything lest his own sin be thrown back up in his face. But, parents, that will always be the case! Every time any child does wrong, if they know that you have ever done anything similar, they will throw that back up at you. And when they do, silence and passivity is never the right response. The right response is, "Yes, I did wrong, and I love you enough to do whatever I have to do to make sure you don't go the way I went!"

Parents, DO stand against your children's wickedness, for their own benefit, even if it means having to re-face what you used to be and do!

Personal Notes:

_____

_____

_____

_____

_____

_____

_____

_____

_____

_____

_____

_____

_____

_____

_____

_____

_____

_____

_____

_____

_____

_____

_____

_____

_____

Devotion 41

After two full years, Absalom took revenge on his half brother, Amnon, for raping his sister Tamar. He invited him and all of the other of the king's children to a party. He specifically pressed for Amnon to be there, and David allowed it.

Partway through the party, Absalom had his servants murder Amnon. When word got back to David, the information was wrong; David was told that all of his sons were dead. He immediately tore his clothes and fell on the ground, mourning.

But there was one man who knew better:

2 Samuel 13:32 *And Jonadab, the son of Shimeah David's brother, answered and said, Let not my lord suppose that they have slain all the young men the king's sons; for Amnon only is dead: for by the appointment of Absalom this hath been determined from the day that he forced his sister Tamar.*

Jonadab; does that name sound familiar? That would be the exact same Jonadab who told Amnon exactly how to do what he did to his sister. This was Amnon's "friend." This "friend" told him how to commit the most horrible of sins, and then sat back quietly and waited for him to be murdered because of it.

This is why every one of us should be so careful who we choose as our friends, and it is also why parents should very actively screen the potential friends of their children!

DO take an active role and a godly approach to choosing and allowing friends; in many ways, a person's friends, for good or bad, will be the most influential people in their lives!

Personal Notes:

_____

_____

_____

_____

_____

_____

_____

_____

_____

_____

_____

_____

_____

_____

_____

_____

_____

_____

_____

_____

_____

_____

_____

_____

_____

_____

_____

Devotion 42

David had been told that all of his sons were dead. But Jonadab, the creep who helped start this whole sorry mess, assured him that it was just Amnon that had been murdered by Absalom. And sure enough, when David saw folks coming back from the party that turned out to be true.

2 Samuel 13:36 *And it came to pass, as soon as he had made an end of speaking, that, behold, the king's sons came, and lifted up their voice and wept: and the king also and all his servants wept very sore.*

The only one dead was Amnon; so he is what all of the crying was about. And that is what makes something that comes next so very interesting.

2 Samuel 13:37 *But Absalom fled, and went to Talmai, the son of Ammihud, king of Geshur. And David mourned for his son every day.* **38** *So Absalom fled, and went to Geshur, and was there three years.* **39** *And the soul of king David longed to go forth unto Absalom: for he was comforted concerning Amnon, seeing he was dead.*

Absalom fled the country lest he should be put to death as a murderer. In that context, and in that verse, we find that "David mourned for his son every day." It was not Amnon he was mourning over, it was Absalom! In verse thirty-nine we find the odd phrase, "for he was comforted concerning Amnon, seeing he was dead." In other words, David initially mourned for his rapist son when he died, but eventually took comfort in the very fact that he was dead!

How can that be? David, as the king, the chief law officer of the land, was compelled by the law of Moses to put Amnon his son to death for what he did,

Deuteronomy 22:25. But he did not do so. He let things slide for three years, and then took comfort when someone else did in an unjust manner what he should have done in a righteous manner.

He passed the buck. And that passing of the buck is what sent Absalom over the edge, and eventually set him against his own father.

DO take responsibility; it is actually a great deal easier than having to deal with the fallout from not taking responsibility!

Personal Notes:

_____

_____

_____

_____

_____

_____

_____

_____

_____

_____

_____

_____

_____

_____

_____

_____

_____

_____

_____

_____

_____

_____

Devotion 43

In 2 Samuel 14, Absalom was brought back to David. But as chapter fifteen began, David was on the verge of losing his life to him, let alone his kingdom, and he did not even realize it. But as with so many things throughout history, the tiniest things often make the biggest difference.

2 Samuel 15:13 *And there came a messenger to David, saying, The hearts of the men of Israel are after Absalom.*

Here is your trivia quiz for the day: what was this man's name? Isaac? Judah? Eli? Cletus?

We have no idea and will never know until we get to heaven. But one unnamed messenger brought David the warning that saved his life and ultimately the entire kingdom! This anonymous person literally turned the tide and saved everyone.

Yet we do not know who he was. He was just some person who did one small, yet incomprehensibly important thing.

Don't ever think that the small things do not matter; they do! So always DO all of the small things you ought to do and can do, every single day, whether anyone will ever know your name or not. I guarantee you that the one person who never forgot this person was King David!

Personal Notes:

_____
_____
_____
_____
_____
_____
_____
_____
_____
_____
_____
_____
_____
_____
_____
_____
_____
_____
_____
_____
_____
_____
_____
_____
_____
_____
_____
_____
_____

Devotion 44

For a good many years David had lived in the luxury of the palace. No doubt he enjoyed it after spending so many years on the run from King Saul, living in caves, and sleeping on the ground. But suddenly and utterly unexpectedly, David found himself on the run yet again:

2 Samuel 15:14 *And David said unto all his servants that were with him at Jerusalem, Arise, and let us flee; for we shall not else escape from Absalom: make speed to depart, lest he overtake us suddenly, and bring evil upon us, and smite the city with the edge of the sword.* **15** *And the king's servants said unto the king, Behold, thy servants are ready to do whatsoever my lord the king shall appoint.*

David absolutely never expected this. He had babied Absalom, doted on him, refrained from ever punishing him, and now that same Absalom was on his way there to kill him. David was completely blindsided. One minute he was on the throne, the next minute he and his servants were running for their lives.

Life has a way of doing that, doesn't it? The only thing utterly predictable about life is the fact that it is unpredictable! And it is for that very reason we need to lay hold on the one thing that never changes. **Psalm 46:1** says, "*God is our refuge and strength, a very present help in trouble.*" the same God that David ran to for a refuge when fleeing from Saul is the same God that he ran to for refuge when fleeing from his own son.

DO realize that the one thing that never changes is the one thing that we most need not to change; God is always our refuge and strength, a very present help in trouble!

Personal Notes:

_____

_____

_____

_____

_____

_____

_____

_____

_____

_____

_____

_____

_____

_____

_____

_____

_____

_____

_____

_____

_____

_____

_____

_____

_____

_____

_____

_____

Devotion 45

Joshua fought the battle of Jericho, Noah built the ark, Daniel went into the lion's den, Peter walked on water, and Ittai...

Wait, what? Or rather, who? We know all of those other guys, those "heroes," but who is this "Ittai guy?" Just one of the greatest men in the Bible, that's who.

2 Samuel 15:18 *And all his servants passed on beside him; and all the Cherethites, and all the Pelethites, and all the Gittites, six hundred men which came after him from Gath, passed on before the king.* **19** *Then said the king to Ittai the Gittite, Wherefore goest thou also with us? return to thy place, and abide with the king: for thou art a stranger, and also an exile.* **20** *Whereas thou camest but yesterday, should I this day make thee go up and down with us? seeing I go whither I may, return thou, and take back thy brethren: mercy and truth be with thee.* **21** *And Ittai answered the king, and said, As the LORD liveth, and as my lord the king liveth, surely in what place my lord the king shall be, whether in death or life, even there also will thy servant be.*

Exactly one day before David ended up on the run for his life, a guy named Ittai showed up, and he was a Philistine from Goliath's home town! He came to follow David, no doubt making himself persona non grata back in his country.

But twenty-four hours later David was not on the throne; he was running into the wilderness for his life. He saw Ittai, realized the awful predicament this newcomer was in and told him just to stay in the palace with Absalom.

But Ittai did not come for the palace; he came for the king.

DO make up your mind that following the King of kings is not about the mansion or the street of gold but about the King Himself! Those who follow for the palace are not real followers anyway, but those that follow through the wilderness will one day get both the King and the palace!

Personal Notes:

_____

_____

_____

_____

_____

_____

_____

_____

_____

_____

_____

_____

_____

_____

_____

_____

_____

_____

_____

_____

_____

_____

_____

Devotion 46

As David and his servants fled from Jerusalem, a very special group of people were there carrying a very special object:

2 Samuel 15:23 *And all the country wept with a loud voice, and all the people passed over: the king also himself passed over the brook Kidron, and all the people passed over, toward the way of the wilderness.* **24** *And lo Zadok also, and all the Levites were with him, bearing the ark of the covenant of God: and they set down the ark of God; and Abiathar went up, until all the people had done passing out of the city.* **25** *And the king said unto Zadok, Carry back the ark of God into the city: if I shall find favour in the eyes of the LORD, he will bring me again, and shew me both it, and his habitation:*

Many years earlier facing a battle of extermination, Israel did the unthinkable. They carried the ark of God to the conflict and lost it to the Philistines. It was David himself more than sixty years later who finally brought it back to where it needed to be. But now David himself was facing a battle of extermination. And yet in the midst of that battle he had the presence of mind not to make the mistake of previous generations. He told the priest to carry the ark of God back into the city; he would not have it dragged through the wilderness as some kind of a "good luck charm" in his troubles.

That is called "a proper respect for God and the things of God."

DO make up your mind that in good times, bad times, average times, all the time, you will treat God and the things of God with proper respect!

Personal Notes:

_____
_____
_____
_____
_____
_____
_____
_____
_____
_____
_____
_____
_____
_____
_____
_____
_____
_____
_____
_____
_____
_____
_____
_____
_____
_____
_____
_____
_____

Devotion 47

As David fled from the city, bad news continued to rain down on him.

2 Samuel 15:31 *And one told David, saying, Ahithophel is among the conspirators with Absalom. And David said, O LORD, I pray thee, turn the counsel of Ahithophel into foolishness.*

Realizing how shrewd and influential Ahithophel was, David realized he was in big trouble. If Absalom listened to Ahithophel, David knew he would soon be dead. So he prayed for God to turn the counsel of Ahithophel into foolishness. And one verse later...

2 Samuel 15:32 *And it came to pass, that when David was come to the top of the mount, where he worshipped God, behold, Hushai the Archite came to meet him with his coat rent, and earth upon his head:* **33** *Unto whom David said, If thou passest on with me, then thou shalt be a burden unto me:* **34** *But if thou return to the city, and say unto Absalom, I will be thy servant, O king; as I have been thy father's servant hitherto, so will I now also be thy servant: then mayest thou for me defeat the counsel of Ahithophel.*

Hushai was a friend to David, and, like Ahithophel, he was a counselor. So David sent him back into the city to pretend to be following Absalom and to fight against the counsel of Ahithophel.

David prayed for one thing; God sent him something different.

But it worked.

DO understand that God will often give us something different from what we ask for to accomplish the same purpose for which we are praying!

Personal Notes:

_____

_____

_____

_____

_____

_____

_____

_____

_____

_____

_____

_____

_____

_____

_____

_____

_____

_____

_____

_____

_____

_____

_____

_____

_____

_____

_____

_____

_____

_____

Devotion 48

Let me show you a "Hallmark Moment" that isn't.

2 Samuel 16:1 *And when David was a little past the top of the hill, behold, Ziba the servant of Mephibosheth met him, with a couple of asses saddled, and upon them two hundred loaves of bread, and an hundred bunches of raisins, and an hundred of summer fruits, and a bottle of wine. 2 And the king said unto Ziba, What meanest thou by these? And Ziba said, The asses be for the king's household to ride on; and the bread and summer fruit for the young men to eat; and the wine, that such as be faint in the wilderness may drink. 3 And the king said, And where is thy master's son? And Ziba said unto the king, Behold, he abideth at Jerusalem: for he said, To day shall the house of Israel restore me the kingdom of my father. 4 Then said the king to Ziba, Behold, thine are all that pertained unto Mephibosheth. And Ziba said, I humbly beseech thee that I may find grace in thy sight, my lord, O king.*

I cannot tell you how many times I have heard people praise Ziba, and even make him out to be a picture of the Holy Ghost! There is just one problem; he was a rat fink. He was rolling the dice and gambling that David was going to come out on top in this conflict, and assuming that if he threw Mephibosheth (who was paralyzed and could not come to David without Ziba's help anyway) under the bus, David would reward him handsomely.

And he did. But Mephibosheth mourned every day David was away and did not shave until he returned.

DO understand that people will often put on Oscar-winning performances of righteousness when they are really devils inside. And if you do two things, one, follow the money, and two, take a long term view of the situation, you will almost always be able to figure out the truth.

Personal Notes:

_____

_____

_____

_____

_____

_____

_____

_____

_____

_____

_____

_____

_____

_____

_____

_____

_____

_____

_____

_____

_____

_____

_____

_____

Devotion 49

As David and his servants continue to march away from the city, they were accosted by an early, crude, version of Ernest T. Bass.

2 Samuel 16:5 *And when king David came to Bahurim, behold, thence came out a man of the family of the house of Saul, whose name was Shimei, the son of Gera: he came forth, and cursed still as he came.* **6** *And he cast stones at David, and at all the servants of king David: and all the people and all the mighty men were on his right hand and on his left.* **7** *And thus said Shimei when he cursed, Come out, come out, thou bloody man, and thou man of Belial:* **8** *The LORD hath returned upon thee all the blood of the house of Saul, in whose stead thou hast reigned; and the LORD hath delivered the kingdom into the hand of Absalom thy son: and, behold, thou art taken in thy mischief, because thou art a bloody man.*

This cursing, rock-throwing, loudmouth punk couched everything he did and said in terms of "righteous indignation." The only problem was, everything he said was an absolute lie, there was no truth to it whatsoever.

For David, the timing could not have been worse. This was salt in the wound, kicking a man when he was down. But isn't that always the devil's favorite time to do something like this?

But here is a spoiler alert for you; it wasn't many days later that Shimei found himself groveling for mercy at David's feet.

DO understand that God is in the habit of settling the scores that we in righteous forbearance leave in His hands to settle!

Personal Notes:

_____
_____
_____
_____
_____
_____
_____
_____
_____
_____
_____
_____
_____
_____
_____
_____
_____
_____
_____
_____
_____
_____
_____
_____
_____
_____
_____
_____
_____
_____

Devotion 50

Back in the palace, Absalom had arrived to take his father's throne. He immediately asked counsel of Ahithophel, and Ahithophel gave wicked, yet very effective counsel. He told Absalom to spread a tent on the top of the roof, and in the sight of all Israel defile his own father's concubines.

Doing this let everyone know that there could be no reconciliation, and they had to choose one side or the other.

That wicked deed done, further counsel was asked of Ahithophel, and once again his counsel, humanly speaking, was good. He told Absalom to let him take 12,000 men to immediately pursue after David. Had he done so, David would never have survived.

But then they asked counsel of Hushai, David's friend and spy in the palace. Hushai intentionally gave horrible counsel. His advice was to gather the entire nation together to pursue after David. That would take a tremendous amount of time and would give David time to prepare for the coming attack. Anyone with any good sense could have seen that. So how did Hushai get Absalom to go along with such poor counsel?

Simple; he played to his pride. **2 Samuel 16:11** *"and that thou go to battle in thine own person."* In other words, "If you are there actually at the fight, Absalom, you will get all the glory from it!"

Absalom knew nothing of war. But his pride clouded his good judgment, and cost him his life.

DO be willing to admit when you do not know something or cannot do something; the humble can be helped, but the proud cannot help but ultimately be hurt!

Personal Notes:

_____

_____

_____

_____

_____

_____

_____

_____

_____

_____

_____

_____

_____

_____

_____

_____

_____

_____

_____

_____

_____

_____

_____

_____

_____

_____

_____

_____

Devotion 51

Hushai sent word to David of what Ahithophel had counseled, and how he had counseled against it. He told David and his men to run just in case.

The two young men that he sent this warning to David by were Jonathan and Ahimaaz. They put their lives at risk to get David this message. And sure enough, a young man saw them and brought word to Absalom that something nefarious was afoot. Absalom sent people after them, and it is then that we read of a remarkable rescue.

2 Samuel 17:18 *Nevertheless a lad saw them, and told Absalom: but they went both of them away quickly, and came to a man's house in Bahurim, which had a well in his court; whither they went down.* **19** *And the woman took and spread a covering over the well's mouth, and spread ground corn thereon; and the thing was not known.* **20** *And when Absalom's servants came to the woman to the house, they said, Where is Ahimaaz and Jonathan? And the woman said unto them, They be gone over the brook of water. And when they had sought and could not find them, they returned to Jerusalem.*

These two men were dangling at the end of a rope down in the well, in utter darkness. The mouth of the well had been covered, and ground corn spread all over it to make it look just like the rest of the barnyard. This was adventure and intrigue, it was people risking their lives to do what was right.

We do not know the name of this woman who saved Ahimaaz and Jonathan. But I guarantee you they never forgot her.

Had those men been found, not only would they have been killed, she would have been killed for trying to hide them.

Doing right is sometimes very scary and very risky, but always, always, always DO right!

Personal Notes:

_____

_____

_____

_____

_____

_____

_____

_____

_____

_____

_____

_____

_____

_____

_____

_____

_____

_____

_____

_____

_____

_____

_____

_____

_____

Devotion 52

We now come to one of the most poignant and downright sad verses in the Bible.

2 Samuel 17:23 *And when Ahithophel saw that his counsel was not followed, he saddled his ass, and arose, and gat him home to his house, to his city, and put his household in order, and hanged himself, and died, and was buried in the sepulchre of his father.*

Ahithophel had once been David's most trusted advisor. But when David did what he did to and with Bathsheba, his granddaughter, and Uriah, his valiant grandson-in-law, he could never look at David the same way again. So when Absalom revolted against David, Ahithophel, seeing a chance for revenge, joined with Absalom.

And yet Absalom rejected his counsel. At that point, Ahithophel knew that David was going to win and also decided that his life had no meaning since his counsel had been rejected.

Ahithophel did wrong in response to wrong, but his wrong was still wrong. He chose to align himself with Absalom who was far more wicked than David as a response to David's wickedness. David repented of his wrongdoing; Absalom never did.

Wrong is always wrong even if it is done as a response to another wrong. If you want to live long and have a life blessed by God, DO right no matter what wrong others have done!

Personal Notes:

_____
_____
_____
_____
_____
_____
_____
_____
_____
_____
_____
_____
_____
_____
_____
_____
_____
_____
_____
_____
_____
_____
_____
_____
_____
_____
_____
_____
_____

Devotion 53

Have you ever considered the power of "and"? Observe the following verses which describe some great men bringing refreshment to David and his weary servants in their great hour of need.

2 Samuel 17:27 *And it came to pass, when David was come to Mahanaim, that Shobi the son of Nahash of Rabbah of the children of Ammon, and Machir the son of Ammiel of Lodebar, and Barzillai the Gileadite of Rogelim,* **28** *Brought beds, and basons, and earthen vessels, and wheat, and barley, and flour, and parched corn, and beans, and lentiles, and parched pulse,* **29** *And honey, and butter, and sheep, and cheese of kine, for David, and for the people that were with him, to eat: for they said, The people is hungry, and weary, and thirsty, in the wilderness.*

In the list of supplies given in verses twenty-eight and twenty-nine, we read the word "and" thirteen times! If a grammar teacher were grading that sentence, she would tell the student to take out all of those ands and just utilize commas instead.

But God put all of those ands in there for a reason. It was His way of pointing out that He noticed every single thing that these men did for David, He noticed every detail of their generosity and kindness.

Do you sometimes feel like God does not notice the things you do? Not only does He notice those deeds of kindness and generosity, He ANDS them. DO remind yourself every day that even if the world does not know what you do, God does!

Personal Notes:

_____

_____

_____

_____

_____

_____

_____

_____

_____

_____

_____

_____

_____

_____

_____

_____

_____

_____

_____

_____

_____

_____

_____

_____

_____

_____

_____

_____

Devotion 54

David and his men set up shop in the city of Mahanaim, a Levitical city in the territory of Gad to the east of the Jordan River. It was there that he began to organize his forces for the coming battle. But as his men were getting ready to march away and fight for him, David gave a command based solely out of emotion and devoid of any good sense whatsoever.

2 Samuel 18:5 *And the king commanded Joab and Abishai and Ittai, saying, Deal gently for my sake with the young man, even with Absalom. And all the people heard when the king gave all the captains charge concerning Absalom.*

Joab and Abishai and Ittai were the captains over the three divisions of David's army, at least what was left of it after Absalom's revolt. He told those men in everyone's hearing to "deal gently with Absalom."

Deal gently with Absalom? Absalom was literally trying to kill David. Absalom would not have hesitated to kill Joab and Abishai and Ittai and every single person following them. David was asking his men to try and handle a rattlesnake with soft cotton gloves.

Emotion makes a terrible guide. Whenever there are important decisions to be made, DO set emotion to the side and consult facts instead!

Personal Notes:

_____

_____

_____

_____

_____

_____

_____

_____

_____

_____

_____

_____

_____

_____

_____

_____

_____

_____

_____

_____

_____

_____

_____

_____

_____

_____

Devotion 55

As the battle was joined, Absalom quickly found out that war is no place for "pretty boys."

2 Samuel 18:6 *So the people went out into the field against Israel: and the battle was in the wood of Ephraim; 7 Where the people of Israel were slain before the servants of David, and there was there a great slaughter that day of twenty thousand men. 8 For the battle was there scattered over the face of all the country: and the wood devoured more people that day than the sword devoured. 9 And Absalom met the servants of David. And Absalom rode upon a mule, and the mule went under the thick boughs of a great oak, and his head caught hold of the oak, and he was taken up between the heaven and the earth; and the mule that was under him went away.*

Remember that Absalom had long beautiful hair. That is great for a magazine but horrible for a soldier. He ended up getting tangled in the thick boughs of an oak tree, and the mule that he was riding on just kept on going! So there he was, hanging like a human Christmas ornament, totally helpless in the battle.

DO understand that "pretty" is pretty useless on a man! It is good for man to keep himself as handsome as possible for his wife, but Absalom would have been the original selfie king. He was a diva, and he ended up dead because of that diva-icity!

Personal Notes:

Devotion 56

After Absalom found himself yanked up into a tree by his head, one of David's men saw him hanging there and went and told Joab. The exchange that took place at that point is interesting:

2 Samuel 18:11 *And Joab said unto the man that told him, And, behold, thou sawest him, and why didst thou not smite him there to the ground? and I would have given thee ten shekels of silver, and a girdle.* **12** *And the man said unto Joab, Though I should receive a thousand shekels of silver in mine hand, yet would I not put forth mine hand against the king's son: for in our hearing the king charged thee and Abishai and Ittai, saying, Beware that none touch the young man Absalom.* **13** *Otherwise I should have wrought falsehood against mine own life: for there is no matter hid from the king, and thou thyself wouldest have set thyself against me.*

In life, you will find people that are naive and gullible, and then from time to time, you will find people who are perceptive and careful. This unnamed man was perceptive and careful. He told Joab, *"Otherwise I should have wrought falsehood against mine own life: for there is no matter hid from the king, and thou thyself wouldest have set thyself against me."*

That last part is the most telling. This guy knew the lying, deadly character of Joab! Others may have forgotten what he did to Abner, among other treachery, but this man did not.

DO realize that what people say and what they do are quite often two different things, and liars are often the most polished, persuasive speakers around.

Be in the habit of "putting people on mute" and focusing on their actual behavior!

Personal Notes:

_____

_____

_____

_____

_____

_____

_____

_____

_____

_____

_____

_____

_____

_____

_____

_____

_____

_____

_____

_____

_____

_____

_____

_____

_____

_____

_____

_____

_____

_____

_____

_____

Devotion 57

The end of Absalom was a violent end to a pampered yet deadly and filthy life.

2 Samuel 18:14 *Then said Joab, I may not tarry thus with thee. And he took three darts in his hand, and thrust them through the heart of Absalom, while he was yet alive in the midst of the oak.* **15** *And ten young men that bare Joab's armour compassed about and smote Absalom, and slew him.*

Joab took three darts and thrust them through Absalom's heart. He then stood back as his ten armor-bearers finished the job of putting Absalom to death. What horror it must have been for Absalom in those few seconds to realize that rather than being king, he was about to be dead! He probably expected his father to be soft and command that he be treated gently (which he did), but he found out that Joab felt no particular need to obey that direct command.

He died hanging helpless in a tree while others took his life. Sin has a way of rendering people helpless and then allowing the devil to sit back and watch with glee as they are destroyed.

Once you are "hanging helpless in sin's tree" it is often too late. The best time to avoid this kind of a deadly dilemma is before you ever start down that pathway. DO right, all day every day, and you will not find yourself ruined by your own poor choices!

Personal Notes:

_____
_____
_____
_____
_____
_____
_____
_____
_____
_____
_____
_____
_____
_____
_____
_____
_____
_____
_____
_____
_____
_____
_____
_____
_____

Devotion 58

Absalom was dead, and his burial was quick and inglorious.

2 Samuel 18:17 *And they took Absalom, and cast him into a great pit in the wood, and laid a very great heap of stones upon him: and all Israel fled every one to his tent.* **18** *Now Absalom in his lifetime had taken and reared up for himself a pillar, which is in the king's dale: for he said, I have no son to keep my name in remembrance: and he called the pillar after his own name: and it is called unto this day, Absalom's place.*

At one point Absalom had had three sons. Now they were all apparently dead. Absalom, figuring that no one would remember his name after the death of his sons, built a monument to himself, and named it after himself.

May I make an observation? If you are having to build a monument to yourself to get people to remember you, you probably have not lived much of a worthwhile life! People do not easily forget those who have been kind, godly, faithful, and generous.

Absalom did not build a life, so instead, he built a monument. DO determine, every day that you live, to build a life worth remembering; leave the monument building to others!

Personal Notes:

Devotion 59

Modern young people would be aghast to know that in Bible days there was no texting, calling, messaging, nothing. When word had to be gotten from one person to another, it came by means of "the ankle express."

2 Samuel 18:21 *Then said Joab to Cushi, Go tell the king what thou hast seen. And Cushi bowed himself unto Joab, and ran.* **22** *Then said Ahimaaz the son of Zadok yet again to Joab, But howsoever, let me, I pray thee, also run after Cushi. And Joab said, Wherefore wilt thou run, my son, seeing that thou hast no tidings ready?* **23** *But howsoever, said he, let me run. And he said unto him, Run. Then Ahimaaz ran by the way of the plain, and overran Cushi.*

There was one message to give, and now there were two runners. Ahimaaz was the faster of the two, but he had nothing substantive to say. Look how that played out.

2 Samuel 18:29 *And the king said, Is the young man Absalom safe? And Ahimaaz answered, When Joab sent the king's servant, and me thy servant, I saw a great tumult, but I knew not what it was.*

He got there first and had nothing of value to say. Cushi, who arrived later, was able to give a full, accurate message.

If a person is going to be a preacher or Bible teacher, the one thing they should never be is "an unprepared messenger!" If you expect to be helpful in ministry, DO "sit and learn" before you "run and say!"

Personal Notes:

_____

_____

_____

_____

_____

_____

_____

_____

_____

_____

_____

_____

_____

_____

_____

_____

_____

_____

_____

_____

_____

_____

_____

_____

_____

_____

_____

_____

Devotion 60

Absalom was dead. Damage over, right? Wrong.

2 Samuel 19:9 *And all the people were at strife throughout all the tribes of Israel, saying, The king saved us out of the hand of our enemies, and he delivered us out of the hand of the Philistines; and now he is fled out of the land for Absalom.* **10** *And Absalom, whom we anointed over us, is dead in battle. Now therefore why speak ye not a word of bringing the king back?*

The people were divided, fussing, fighting, not sure what to do now. Most of them had followed Absalom in his rebellion. Even Judah, David's own tribe, was disloyal to him. But look how David handled the situation.

2 Samuel 19:11 *And king David sent to Zadok and to Abiathar the priests, saying, Speak unto the elders of Judah, saying, Why are ye the last to bring the king back to his house? seeing the speech of all Israel is come to the king, even to his house.* **12** *Ye are my brethren, ye are my bones and my flesh: wherefore then are ye the last to bring back the king?...* **14** *And he bowed the heart of all the men of Judah, even as the heart of one man; so that they sent this word unto the king, Return thou, and all thy servants.*

David "bowed their hearts with his words." David, rather than rattling the saber, spoke peaceful, unifying words to a divided people. There is quite a lesson in that!

When a battle is done and the dust is settling, DO be willing to forgive past wrongs. Let bygones be bygones, and speak words of unity rather than words of further division. The need to "settle every score" leaves everyone sitting on zero!

Personal Notes:

_____

_____

_____

_____

_____

_____

_____

_____

_____

_____

_____

_____

_____

_____

_____

_____

_____

_____

_____

_____

_____

_____

_____

_____

_____

_____

_____

_____

_____

Devotion 61

When David finally came back into his kingdom, he was met by an intentionally unkempt individual. Ziba had lied about Mephibosheth, slandering him to David. But from the very day David ran from the palace until the day he returned, verse twenty-four tells us that Mephibosheth had not put shoes on his feet or trimmed his beard or even washed his clothes. This lame individual who had been rescued by David wanted everyone to know that he was loyal to David. This very well could have cost him his life to Absalom.

And yet God preserved him, and the king was able to see for himself the evidence that Mephibosheth was not at all as Ziba had slandered him.

When Ziba first slandered Mephibosheth to David, David gave him all of the property of Mephibosheth. Now, not sure what to do, he simply divided the property between the two of them. Look at how Mephibosheth responded.

2 Samuel 19:30 *And Mephibosheth said unto the king, Yea, let him take all, forasmuch as my lord the king is come again in peace unto his own house.*

Mephibosheth didn't want the stuff; he wanted his savior.

No matter how much God blesses us, DO understand that the blessings are of far less value than the Blesser!

Personal Notes:

Devotion 62

As David was coming over Jordan, a precious old man was with him.

2 Samuel 19:31 *And Barzillai the Gileadite came down from Rogelim, and went over Jordan with the king, to conduct him over Jordan.* **32** *Now Barzillai was a very aged man, even fourscore years old: and he had provided the king of sustenance while he lay at Mahanaim; for he was a very great man.* **33** *And the king said unto Barzillai, Come thou over with me, and I will feed thee with me in Jerusalem.* **34** *And Barzillai said unto the king, How long have I to live, that I should go up with the king unto Jerusalem?* **35** *I am this day fourscore years old: and can I discern between good and evil? can thy servant taste what I eat or what I drink? can I hear any more the voice of singing men and singing women? wherefore then should thy servant be yet a burden unto my lord the king?*

Barzillai was there for David in his hour of greatest need. David offered to bring him to Jerusalem with him and let him live there for the rest of his days. Barzillai kindly refused, and sent his servant, Chimham, instead. Barzillai did not sin in doing so, but he did sell himself short. He told David in so many words, "I am eighty: I cannot be a help to you."

And yet no one in all of this had been a greater help to David than Barzillai, and there is no reason to think he could not have continued to do so.

DO live and serve until the second you die. Way too many people put it in park when they could be dropping down a gear and continuing to pull the load for the Lord!

Personal Notes:

_____
_____
_____
_____
_____
_____
_____
_____
_____
_____
_____
_____
_____
_____
_____
_____
_____
_____
_____
_____
_____
_____
_____
_____
_____
_____
_____
_____

Devotion 63

At the end of 2 Samuel 19, while David was on his way back to Jerusalem, yet another conflict broke out, this time between the tribe of Judah and all of the rest of the tribes of Israel. The other tribes were upset that Judah had not called them to conduct the king back over Jordan. There was a war of words that ensued, and yet as the chapter ended there was no indication that there would be any further trouble. It was simply a personality conflict, something that could easily be gotten past. Until, that is, yet another loud-mouthed rabble-rouser jumped into the fray:

2 Samuel 20:1 *And there happened to be there a man of Belial, whose name was Sheba, the son of Bichri, a Benjamite: and he blew a trumpet, and said, We have no part in David, neither have we inheritance in the son of Jesse: every man to his tents, O Israel. 2 So every man of Israel went up from after David, and followed Sheba the son of Bichri: but the men of Judah clave unto their king, from Jordan even to Jerusalem.*

Give a man a trumpet, a big mouth, and a rotten attitude, and there is no telling the damage he can cause. In this case, it was yet another split in the kingdom, just as everything was starting to heal. And who was this guy, Sheba, and what were his qualifications to determine how the kingdom should go?

Just one: he was distantly related to the former king. In other words, he was a nobody who thought he was a somebody and was willing to tell everybody. This kind of person is always the wrong kind of person to listen to, in anything!

DO pay more attention to substance than to volume. A trumpet and a big mouth are no substitute for the anointing of God or for a track record of success!

Personal Notes:

_____

_____

_____

_____

_____

_____

_____

_____

_____

_____

_____

_____

_____

_____

_____

_____

_____

_____

_____

_____

_____

_____

_____

_____

_____

_____

_____

Devotion 64

After Sheba started the newest rebellion, David commanded his newly installed general, Amasa, to gather the men of Judah, be back in three days time, and go deal with Sheba. Amasa was newly in charge, Joab having been put out of that position by David.

But Amasa was not back in time. So David quickly went with plan B, sending Abishai and some men to go after Sheba. Joab, spurned for a second time, went along with Abishai. But along the way, they ran into Amasa. When they did, and I know this will come as a total shock to you, Joab murdered him in cold blood.

2 Samuel 20:9 *And Joab said to Amasa, Art thou in health, my brother? And Joab took Amasa by the beard with the right hand to kiss him.* **10** *But Amasa took no heed to the sword that was in Joab's hand: so he smote him therewith in the fifth rib, and shed out his bowels to the ground, and struck him not again; and he died. So Joab and Abishai his brother pursued after Sheba the son of Bichri.*

Who could have seen that coming?

With Joab, anyone with a single functioning brain cell.

DO pay attention to the patterns people establish in their behavior. Joab spoke words of peace and kindness, and then murdered the man he was speaking to. People say lots of things; but if the patterns of their life say otherwise, it would be best not to let them get too close!

Personal Notes:

_____
_____
_____
_____
_____
_____
_____
_____
_____
_____
_____
_____
_____
_____
_____
_____
_____
_____
_____
_____
_____
_____
_____
_____
_____
_____
_____
_____
_____

Devotion 65

As Joab and the army he gathered pursued after Sheba, they finally cornered him in a town called Abel. Joab and his men besieged the city, and it is clear they had every intention of leveling it to the ground. But by the time the day was over the city was saved and only Sheba was dead. How in the world did that happen, and who was responsible for it?

2 Samuel 20:16 *Then cried a wise woman out of the city, Hear, hear; say, I pray you, unto Joab, Come near hither, that I may speak with thee.*

A woman. A wise woman. After finding out from Joab what the problem was, here is what she did.

2 Samuel 20:21b... *And the woman said unto Joab, Behold, his head shall be thrown to thee over the wall.* **22** *Then the woman went unto all the people in her wisdom. And they cut off the head of Sheba the son of Bichri, and cast it out to Joab. And he blew a trumpet, and they retired from the city, every man to his tent. And Joab returned to Jerusalem unto the king.*

The city was saved by the wisdom of one woman. And yet we are constantly told that women in the Bible were oppressed and viewed as nothing more than property. The only problem is, page after page of Scripture tells a very different story!

DO know that God has built the potential for greatness into both genders of His creation, and He expects both man and woman to live up to that potential!

Personal Notes:

_____
_____
_____
_____
_____
_____
_____
_____
_____
_____
_____
_____
_____
_____
_____
_____
_____
_____
_____
_____
_____
_____
_____
_____
_____
_____

Devotion 66

2 Samuel 21 is one of the most unusual, and saddest, chapters in the Bible. It begins with a three-year famine during the reign of David. David asked God why it was happening and was informed that it was because of a great sin during the reign of Saul. Saul had, at some point, tried to wipe out the Gibeonites, people that the Children of Israel had made a covenant with that they would spare their lives.

Many decades had passed, and now God was requiring judgment for that sin. David asked the Gibeonites what it would take for them to be satisfied that justice had been done, and the price was steep for the family of Saul; seven of his descendants were to be slain.

In the big scheme of things, seven people being put to death was certainly better than an entire nation starving. But for one woman that was no consolation. Two of the slain were the sons of a mother named Rizpah. This broken-hearted woman, when she could do nothing else, kept vigil over their dead bodies which had been hung:

2 Samuel 21:10 *And Rizpah the daughter of Aiah took sackcloth, and spread it for her upon the rock, from the beginning of harvest until water dropped upon them out of heaven, and suffered neither the birds of the air to rest on them by day, nor the beasts of the field by night.*

This is a mother's heart on display. What a gift God gave humanity when He invented this creature called "mother!" DO treasure your mother, and DO give her the easiest time possible. Her heartbreaks are often unfathomable, yet she, like Rizpah, will likely be the last person to ever leave you no matter what.

Personal Notes:

_____

_____

_____

_____

_____

_____

_____

_____

_____

_____

_____

_____

_____

_____

_____

_____

_____

_____

_____

_____

_____

_____

_____

_____

_____

_____

_____

_____

_____

Devotion 67

David burst onto the scene in 1 Samuel 17 when he killed giant Goliath in battle. But Goliath was not the last giant in that family. At the end of 2 Samuel 21, we find four more giants from that same line having to be killed. And we also find that David himself nearly died trying to do so:

2 Samuel 21:15 *Moreover the Philistines had yet war again with Israel; and David went down, and his servants with him, and fought against the Philistines: and David waxed faint.* **16** *And Ishbibenob, which was of the sons of the giant, the weight of whose spear weighed three hundred shekels of brass in weight, he being girded with a new sword, thought to have slain David.* **17** *But Abishai the son of Zeruiah succoured him, and smote the Philistine, and killed him. Then the men of David sware unto him, saying, Thou shalt go no more out with us to battle, that thou quench not the light of Israel.*

How is it that the same David who killed Goliath had to be rescued when attempting to kill another giant? If you are looking for a deeply spiritual answer on this, you are going to be disappointed.

David got old.

David was a young man full of energy when he killed Goliath. By the time this battle took place with his four brothers, David was old and tired. But does that mean he lost his value? No, in fact, he was of greater value than ever. Previously he had been just a warrior. Now, in the accurate words of his men, he was the very "light of Israel!"

DO understand that as your hair gets gray and your back gets stooped, your value only increases.

You go from being an "up and coming doer" to a living example for all of the other "up and comers." Your strength may be greatly decreased, but your influence is greatly increased!

Personal Notes:

_____
_____
_____
_____
_____
_____
_____
_____
_____
_____
_____
_____
_____
_____
_____
_____
_____
_____
_____
_____
_____
_____
_____
_____
_____
_____
_____
_____

Devotion 68

2 Samuel 23 brings us to David's "last will and testament." And it is at once both beautiful and heartbreaking:

2 Samuel 23:1 *Now these be the last words of David. David the son of Jesse said, and the man who was raised up on high, the anointed of the God of Jacob, and the sweet psalmist of Israel, said,* **2** *The Spirit of the LORD spake by me, and his word was in my tongue.* **3** *The God of Israel said, the Rock of Israel spake to me, He that ruleth over men must be just, ruling in the fear of God.* **4** *And he shall be as the light of the morning, when the sun riseth, even a morning without clouds; as the tender grass springing out of the earth by clear shining after rain.* **5** *Although my house be not so with God; yet he hath made with me an everlasting covenant, ordered in all things, and sure: for this is all my salvation, and all my desire, although he make it not to grow.*

David recognized in verse two that, "*He that ruleth over men must be just, ruling in the fear of God.*" But then he gave the honest acknowledgment in verse five, "Although my house be not so with God..."

David was dying. In his last days, he looked back over his life with an honest gaze and said in so many words, "I wasn't always what I should have been." His affair with Bathsheba and murder of Uriah certainly did not fit under the heading of "just, and ruling in the fear of God."

And yet, the very next phrase was, "*Yet he hath made with me an everlasting covenant, ordered in all things, and sure.*" While David was not always what he said he would be for God, God was always what He said He would be for David!

DO always do right, but DO also always rest in the fact that even when we are not faithful to God, God in His mercy is faithful to us!

Personal Notes:

_____
_____
_____
_____
_____
_____
_____
_____
_____
_____
_____
_____
_____
_____
_____
_____
_____
_____
_____
_____
_____
_____
_____
_____
_____
_____

Devotion 69

After the recounting of David's last will and testament, the rest of 2 Samuel 23 gives us the account of David's 37 mighty men. We have already seen throughout the life of David that he was a mighty warrior and quite capable of handling himself well in a fight. And yet he was also wise enough to realize that he was just one man and that if the kingdom was all about his strength, it would be very limited.

Consider just one of them, a man by the name of Shammah.

2 Samuel 23:11 *And after him was Shammah the son of Agee the Hararite. And the Philistines were gathered together into a troop, where was a piece of ground full of lentiles: and the people fled from the Philistines.* **12** *But he stood in the midst of the ground, and defended it, and slew the Philistines: and the LORD wrought a great victory.*

Like Shammah, all of these mighty men were men who knew how to take a stand and not back down. Because David had the wisdom and humility to seek out and utilize men like that, the kingdom went from a disorganized, weak mess under Saul, to the height of its power under David. Most kingdoms take several generations to even begin to reach their height; with Israel, it was from the lowest of the low to the highest of the high in just one rule, David's. And his mighty men played a vital role in that meteoric rise.

No matter how strong and capable you are in anything, you are still just one person. DO have the wisdom and the humility to draw on the strengths and abilities of others! Doing so unleashes the power of multiplication, while refusing to do so leaves you only with "me plus me equals me." That is very poor math and even worse leadership!

Personal Notes:

_____

_____

_____

_____

_____

_____

_____

_____

_____

_____

_____

_____

_____

_____

_____

_____

_____

_____

_____

_____

_____

_____

_____

_____

_____

_____

_____

_____

_____

_____

Devotion 70

2 Samuel 24 and 1 Chronicles 21 record what appears to be one of the last official acts of David, and it was not a good one. Both of those chapters record the day when David numbered the people of Israel, something that God had very clearly made known that He did not want done at that time.

Having disobeyed, David quickly realized that he was once again in trouble. And yet, when God sent word to him with the options for his punishment, the choice of David is a very instructive one for us.

2 Samuel 24:11 *For when David was up in the morning, the word of the LORD came unto the prophet Gad, David's seer, saying,* **12** *Go and say unto David, Thus saith the LORD, I offer thee three things; choose thee one of them, that I may do it unto thee.* **13** *So Gad came to David, and told him, and said unto him, Shall seven years of famine come unto thee in thy land? or wilt thou flee three months before thine enemies, while they pursue thee? or that there be three days' pestilence in thy land? now advise, and see what answer I shall return to him that sent me.* **14** *And David said unto Gad, I am in a great strait: let us fall now into the hand of the LORD; for his mercies are great: and let me not fall into the hand of man.*

Notice very carefully what David said: "let US fall now into the hand of the LORD; for his mercies are great: and let ME not fall into the hand of man." In the options that God offered, option number two would fall primarily on David, while options one and three would fall on everyone. David chose one of the options that would fall on everyone, not just on himself. This was the king looking out for the king...

144

How very different is our great King, the Lord Jesus Christ! Our King took all of our punishment on Himself that we may go free and be saved. DO honor the King; there has never been another His equal!

Personal Notes:

_____

_____

_____

_____

_____

_____

_____

_____

_____

_____

_____

_____

_____

_____

_____

_____

_____

_____

_____

_____

_____

_____

_____

_____

_____

_____

Devotion 71

As 2 Samuel 24 began, we found that Israel had sinned some unspecified sin, and God was angry with them. David then sinned by numbering the people. The result of these two things was 70,000 people dead. The plague was finally stopped at the threshing floor of a man named Araunah here in 2 Samuel. His other name, Ornan, is recorded in the parallel account of this event in 1 Chronicles 21.

2 Samuel 24:24 *And the king said unto Araunah, Nay; but I will surely buy it of thee at a price: neither will I offer burnt offerings unto the LORD my God of that which doth cost me nothing. So David bought the threshingfloor and the oxen for fifty shekels of silver.* **25** *And David built there an altar unto the LORD, and offered burnt offerings and peace offerings. So the LORD was intreated for the land, and the plague was stayed from Israel.*

It was just a threshing floor, but later it would become so very much more.

2 Chronicles 3:1 *Then Solomon began to build the house of the LORD at Jerusalem in mount Moriah, where the LORD appeared unto David his father, in the place that David had prepared in the threshingfloor of Ornan the Jebusite.*

A place that had once commemorated the ending of a horrible scene of death became the very place that the greatest temple in Israel's history was built.

When you face hardships and tragedy in your life, DO cast a hopeful eye toward the future; our God is very good at using tragedy as the foundation for triumph!

Personal Notes:

_____
_____
_____
_____
_____
_____
_____
_____
_____
_____
_____
_____
_____
_____
_____
_____
_____
_____
_____
_____
_____
_____
_____
_____
_____
_____
_____
_____

Devotion 72

In David's dying days, we find what is, to our modern, western minds, a head-scratching oddity taking place.

1 Kings 1:1 *Now king David was old and stricken in years; and they covered him with clothes, but he gat no heat.* **2** *Wherefore his servants said unto him, Let there be sought for my lord the king a young virgin: and let her stand before the king, and let her cherish him, and let her lie in thy bosom, that my lord the king may get heat.* **3** *So they sought for a fair damsel throughout all the coasts of Israel, and found Abishag a Shunammite, and brought her to the king.* **4** *And the damsel was very fair, and cherished the king, and ministered to him: but the king knew her not.*

David was not able to fulfill any of the physical, intimate activities of a husband to wife. And yet Abishag, a young woman with her life ahead of her, became his wife anyway simply to give him heat and keep him comfortable. Yes, this was another example of the absurdity of polygamy, which was never God's intent for man, but it is also, in this place, a beautiful example of true compassion. Abishag had nothing to gain from this arrangement; she did what she did out of compassion for another.

It is very easy and common for people in our day to be utterly self-centered. But selflessness and compassion are always near and dear to the heart of God! Again, this is no justification of any wrong done in that polygamous culture, but it does speak well of the heart of Abishag and of anyone who thinks of others before they think of themselves.

DO be compassionate and think of others; your tenderness today may be just the "warmth" they need to survive!

Personal Notes:

_____

_____

_____

_____

_____

_____

_____

_____

_____

_____

_____

_____

_____

_____

_____

_____

_____

_____

_____

_____

_____

_____

_____

_____

_____

_____

_____

_____

_____

_____

Devotion 73

If I were to ask you which child of David caused him trouble, your proper response should probably be, "which child DIDN'T cause him trouble?"

1 Kings 1:5 *Then Adonijah the son of Haggith exalted himself, saying, I will be king: and he prepared him chariots and horsemen, and fifty men to run before him.* **6** *And his father had not displeased him at any time in saying, Why hast thou done so? and he also was a very goodly man; and his mother bare him after Absalom.* **7** *And he conferred with Joab the son of Zeruiah, and with Abiathar the priest: and they following Adonijah helped him.* **8** *But Zadok the priest, and Benaiah the son of Jehoiada, and Nathan the prophet, and Shimei, and Rei, and the mighty men which belonged to David, were not with Adonijah.*

Amnon his son raped Tamar his daughter. Absalom stole the kingdom. Now Adonijah was out for the kingdom. David's children had quite a track record of causing him difficulty. Why is that? A common denominator seems to be found in the words of verse six, "And his father had not displeased him at any time..."

This kid got whatever he wanted, whenever he wanted it. He did whatever he wanted to do, good or bad. And not one single time did David ever call him out or punish him for it. He never "displeased him." His fatherhood philosophy was "give baby whatever he wants." And not only did that philosophy cause David endless trouble, it also ruined the very children he was spoiling so lavishly!

DO love your children enough to "displease them" from time to time. A parent that never says, "No," will eventually inevitably find themselves saying, "Oh, no!"

Personal Notes:

_____

_____

_____

_____

_____

_____

_____

_____

_____

_____

_____

_____

_____

_____

_____

_____

_____

_____

_____

_____

_____

_____

_____

_____

_____

_____

_____

Devotion 74

Nathan and Bathsheba came to David and made him aware of Adonijah's plot to take over the kingdom and to put her and Solomon to death. David knew just what to do to stop that plot in its tracks:

1 Kings 1:33 *The king also said unto them, Take with you the servants of your lord, and cause Solomon my son to ride upon mine own mule, and bring him down to Gihon:* **34** *And let Zadok the priest and Nathan the prophet anoint him there king over Israel: and blow ye with the trumpet, and say, God save king Solomon.* **35** *Then ye shall come up after him, that he may come and sit upon my throne; for he shall be king in my stead: and I have appointed him to be ruler over Israel and over Judah.*

The king's "vehicle." The anointing of both Zadok the priest and Nathan the prophet. The throne to sit on. Everything needed to stamp a king as "official" was provided. Adonijah could claim to be king, but Solomon was carrying all of the proof! Lots of people claim lots of things; each and every day a Nigerian prince offers to give me tens of millions of dollars for the low low price of $1000 or so on my part. The "IRS" calls to tell me they are coming for my children if I do not wire them money. "Democratic socialists" offer to give all of us everything for free if we will just vote for them.

But there will never be any substitute for actual facts. As you go about your day, as you turn on the supposedly unbiased news, as you scroll social media, DO refuse to automatically buy what you hear and see. Adonijah put on quite a performance, but

Solomon was riding the king's mule all the way to the throne room!

Personal Notes:

_____

_____

_____

_____

_____

_____

_____

_____

_____

_____

_____

_____

_____

_____

_____

_____

_____

_____

_____

_____

_____

_____

_____

_____

_____

_____

_____

_____

Devotion 75

With Solomon installed on the throne, David in his dying days had some words of counsel for him:

1 Kings 2:1 *Now the days of David drew nigh that he should die; and he charged Solomon his son, saying,* **2** *I go the way of all the earth: be thou strong therefore, and shew thyself a man;* **3** *And keep the charge of the LORD thy God, to walk in his ways, to keep his statutes, and his commandments, and his judgments, and his testimonies, as it is written in the law of Moses, that thou mayest prosper in all that thou doest, and whithersoever thou turnest thyself:*

For believers, the words of verse three should certainly not come as a surprise. It was David's command that Solomon follow the Lord and always do right. But in our day, the words he spoke to him in verse two would certainly come as a surprise to the misguided world around us. David told his son to "be strong and manly."

Perhaps you have noticed that actual manhood is under assault in our day. Phrases like "toxic masculinity" are thrown around to embarrass boys into laying aside masculinity and instead embracing effemininity. Commercials keep appearing telling us that " there is no one way to be a man," and that things like physical strength, bravery, and the willingness to fight for what is right are actually bad things.

The Brawny Paper Towel guy even lost his beard and now looks much more GQ than Carhart.

But God made men to be... manly. And a wise parent will encourage their boys to be just that! Parents, DO encourage all of your children to godliness, but DO also really encourage your boys to manliness!

Personal Notes:

_____

_____

_____

_____

_____

_____

_____

_____

_____

_____

_____

_____

_____

_____

_____

_____

_____

_____

_____

_____

_____

_____

_____

_____

_____

_____

_____

_____

_____

_____

Devotion 76

Just before he died, David made a list of things for Solomon to do:

1 Kings 2:5 *Moreover thou knowest also what Joab the son of Zeruiah did to me, and what he did to the two captains of the hosts of Israel, unto Abner the son of Ner, and unto Amasa the son of Jether, whom he slew, and shed the blood of war in peace, and put the blood of war upon his girdle that was about his loins, and in his shoes that were on his feet.* **6** *Do therefore according to thy wisdom, and let not his hoar head go down to the grave in peace.* **7** *But shew kindness unto the sons of Barzillai the Gileadite, and let them be of those that eat at thy table: for so they came to me when I fled because of Absalom thy brother.* **8** *And, behold, thou hast with thee Shimei the son of Gera, a Benjamite of Bahurim, which cursed me with a grievous curse in the day when I went to Mahanaim: but he came down to meet me at Jordan, and I sware to him by the LORD, saying, I will not put thee to death with the sword.* **9** *Now therefore hold him not guiltless: for thou art a wise man, and knowest what thou oughtest to do unto him; but his hoar head bring thou down to the grave with blood.*

There were three items on this list, and two-thirds of that list were negative. David told Solomon to show kindness to the family of Barzillai. But he also told him to put Joab and Shimei to death. In other words, there were two big problems that David never bothered to deal with and instead left those problems for his son to deal with later. Solomon did deal with them, but how much better would it have been for David to have dealt with them during his own life!

DO make a habit of dealing with your own problems rather than passing them on to others. No matter what the context or situation, it simply isn't fair to shirk our duties and then expect others to clean up the mess!

Personal Notes:

_____

_____

_____

_____

_____

_____

_____

_____

_____

_____

_____

_____

_____

_____

_____

_____

_____

_____

_____

_____

_____

_____

_____

_____

_____

_____

_____

Devotion 77

David was dead, and Solomon his son was now on the throne as the third king of Israel. But as on any chessboard, there are kings and there are pawns. And very early in his reign, an opponent tried to utilize a pawn against him.

1 Kings 2:13 *And Adonijah the son of Haggith came to Bathsheba the mother of Solomon. And she said, Comest thou peaceably? And he said, Peaceably. **14** He said moreover, I have somewhat to say unto thee. And she said, Say on. **15** And he said, Thou knowest that the kingdom was mine, and that all Israel set their faces on me, that I should reign: howbeit the kingdom is turned about, and is become my brother's: for it was his from the LORD. **16** And now I ask one petition of thee, deny me not. And she said unto him, Say on.*

What he asked for seemed innocent enough to Bathsheba:

1 Kings 2:17 *And he said, Speak, I pray thee, unto Solomon the king, (for he will not say thee nay,) that he give me Abishag the Shunammite to wife.*

His opening words, totally focused on his loss of the kingdom, let us know that Adonijah was not in love with Abishag, who had been the wife/warmer of King David; he wanted to use her as a pawn to try and retake the kingdom from his younger brother, Solomon.

This was horribly unfair to Abishag. No person should ever be treated as a pawn.

As you go about your day, DO treat everyone you meet as someone important, never as a pawn to get what you want. Whoever they are, God loved them enough to die for them!

Personal Notes:

_____

_____

_____

_____

_____

_____

_____

_____

_____

_____

_____

_____

_____

_____

_____

_____

_____

_____

_____

_____

_____

_____

_____

_____

_____

_____

_____

_____

_____

Devotion 78

Adonijah was quickly put to death for his transparent attempt to usurp the throne from Solomon by asking for Abishag to be his wife. But there were yet more people on the new king's radar screen that day:

1 Kings 2:22 *And king Solomon answered and said unto his mother, And why dost thou ask Abishag the Shunammite for Adonijah? ask for him the kingdom also; for he is mine elder brother; even for him, and for Abiathar the priest, and for Joab the son of Zeruiah.*

Abiathar had been the priest and a faithful friend to David. Joab had been David's general and the most maddeningly conflicting person in David's life. He had been utterly loyal to David and then would turn around at a split second's notice and defy David, killing some person that David valued.

Both of them, though, had followed after Adonijah.

When it came time for Solomon to deal with them in this new matter of Adonijah, he dealt with them very differently. Joab was put to death while holding onto the very horns of the altar. But here is what Solomon said to Abiathar:

1 Kings 2:26 *And unto Abiathar the priest said the king, Get thee to Anathoth, unto thine own fields; for thou art worthy of death: but I will not at this time put thee to death, because thou barest the ark of the Lord GOD before David my father, and because thou hast been afflicted in all wherein my father was afflicted.*

In 1 Samuel 22, Abiathar's entire family had been slaughtered by Saul out of his hatred for David. Only young Abiathar escaped and came to David. He then spent many loyal decades serving David, running for his life along with David from Saul and then from Absalom. It had only been very recently that he had done wrong in backing Adonijah for king when God and David had chosen Solomon.

Solomon was wise enough to not simply disregard forty plus years of this man's utter loyalty to David over one bad choice. He was rightly put out of the priesthood, but his life was spared, and his good deeds were remembered and recounted,

You will often end up dealing with people who have done right for years and then done wrong. While wrong must never, ever be excused or even minimized, DO also be wise enough to extend grace to people for all of the right they did before they ever did wrong!

Personal Notes:

_____

_____

_____

_____

_____

_____

_____

_____

_____

_____

_____

_____

Devotion 79

Joab was dead, Abiathar was put out of the priesthood, but there was still one more person to be dealt with right at the beginning of Solomon's reign.

1 Kings 2:36 *And the king sent and called for Shimei, and said unto him, Build thee an house in Jerusalem, and dwell there, and go not forth thence any whither.* **37** *For it shall be, that on the day thou goest out, and passest over the brook Kidron, thou shalt know for certain that thou shalt surely die: thy blood shall be upon thine own head.* **38** *And Shimei said unto the king, The saying is good: as my lord the king hath said, so will thy servant do. And Shimei dwelt in Jerusalem many days.*

Shimei was the creep who had thrown rocks and mud and cursed at David when he was running from Jerusalem as Absalom usurped the throne. When David came back victorious, Shimei came back groveling, and David agreed to let him live. But this man, a relative to Saul, and a proven trouble maker, was clearly a threat to Solomon's kingdom. So Solomon commanded that he leave Bahurim, out where he could make trouble among the people, and move into Jerusalem where Solomon could keep an eye on him. The city would be his prison, and what a generous prison that was! Anyone "imprisoned" in the capital city of a land, with the free run of that city, has gotten off easy! But to quote the younger crowd today, "Shimei gonna Shimei."

1 Kings 2:39 *And it came to pass at the end of three years, that two of the servants of Shimei ran away unto Achish son of Maachah king of Gath. And they told Shimei, saying, Behold, thy servants be in*

Gath. **40** *And Shimei arose, and saddled his ass, and went to Gath to Achish to seek his servants: and Shimei went, and brought his servants from Gath.*

Shimei was put to death for this. He disobeyed the clear command of the king and paid the clearly stated price.

DO learn to obey God in all things. Instead of being a "Shimei gonna Shimei," be a "Fill-in-your-name gonna obey!"

Personal Notes:

_____
_____
_____
_____
_____
_____
_____
_____
_____
_____
_____
_____
_____
_____
_____
_____
_____
_____
_____
_____
_____
_____

Devotion 80

Solomon was established on the throne and was worshiping God in spectacular ways:

1 Kings 3:4 *And the king went to Gibeon to sacrifice there; for that was the great high place: a thousand burnt offerings did Solomon offer upon that altar.*

It was at that time that the most important event of Solomon's life took place.

1 Kings 3:5 *In Gibeon the LORD appeared to Solomon in a dream by night: and God said, Ask what I shall give thee.*

This was a blank check drawn on the bank of heaven and signed with God's signature! And yet, with that great blank check, Solomon did not ask for wealth or health or success, he asked for something that cannot be touched, traded, bartered, or leveraged: wisdom. Why would he do that, and where did he come up with such an idea? We do not have to guess, he later wrote down the answer for us:

Proverbs 4:3 *For I was my father's son, tender and only beloved in the sight of my mother.* **4** *He taught me also, and said unto me, Let thine heart retain my words: keep my commandments, and live.* **5** *Get wisdom, get understanding: forget it not; neither decline from the words of my mouth.*

David told Solomon to get wisdom! So when God told him he could have anything he asked for, that is what he asked for.

Parents, DO teach your children what things are truly important so that when their times come to make important choices, they are already prepared to choose all the right things!

Personal Notes:

_____
_____
_____
_____
_____
_____
_____
_____
_____
_____
_____
_____
_____
_____
_____
_____
_____
_____
_____
_____
_____
_____
_____
_____
_____
_____
_____
_____

Devotion 81

God had written Solomon a blank check, and Solomon filled it in with the word "wisdom." Here is how God reacted to that choice on his part:

1 Kings 3:10 *And the speech pleased the Lord, that Solomon had asked this thing.* **11** *And God said unto him, Because thou hast asked this thing, and hast not asked for thyself long life; neither hast asked riches for thyself, nor hast asked the life of thine enemies; but hast asked for thyself understanding to discern judgment;* **12** *Behold, I have done according to thy words: lo, I have given thee a wise and an understanding heart; so that there was none like thee before thee, neither after thee shall any arise like unto thee.* **13** *And I have also given thee that which thou hast not asked, both riches, and honour: so that there shall not be any among the kings like unto thee all thy days.*

Solomon did not ask for the obvious things a king would normally ask for, but in response to what he did ask for, God freely gave him the obvious things as well! Solomon found that when a person seeks what really matters to God, God often turns and gives not just that, but also many other things that matter to man.

How did Jesus put it? **Matthew 6:33** *But seek ye first the kingdom of God, and his righteousness; and all these things shall be added unto you.*

It isn't so much a matter of what we seek, but of what we seek FIRST. When we prioritize seeking after spiritual things, God prioritizes providing temporal things.

If you would like God to meet your needs and then some, DO put the first things first!

Personal Notes:

_____

_____

_____

_____

_____

_____

_____

_____

_____

_____

_____

_____

_____

_____

_____

_____

_____

_____

_____

_____

_____

_____

_____

_____

_____

_____

_____

Devotion 82

Right after Solomon asked for and received wisdom, that wisdom was put to the test in an episode so famous that our modern culture still uses it as a euphemism for figuring out any hard problem.

1 Kings 3:16 *Then came there two women, that were harlots, unto the king, and stood before him.* **17** *And the one woman said, O my lord, I and this woman dwell in one house; and I was delivered of a child with her in the house.* **18** *And it came to pass the third day after that I was delivered, that this woman was delivered also: and we were together; there was no stranger with us in the house, save we two in the house.* **19** *And this woman's child died in the night; because she overlaid it.* **20** *And she arose at midnight, and took my son from beside me, while thine handmaid slept, and laid it in her bosom, and laid her dead child in my bosom.* **21** *And when I rose in the morning to give my child suck, behold, it was dead: but when I had considered it in the morning, behold, it was not my son, which I did bear.* **22** *And the other woman said, Nay; but the living is my son, and the dead is thy son. And this said, No; but the dead is thy son, and the living is my son. Thus they spake before the king.*

We know how the story ended, with Solomon proposing to cut the child in half, knowing that the real mother would never, ever allow that. But may we focus in on that mother for a moment? She was a harlot, and that was a crime punishable by death. And yet she was first willing to risk death to save her child, and then willing to lose her child in order to save his life.

What a rebuke to our abortion worshiping society.

DO know and tell anyone who will listen that precious babes are worth saving and that in our day, we have the lovely option of adoption we can look to instead of the hideous wrong of abortion!

Personal Notes:

_____

_____

_____

_____

_____

_____

_____

_____

_____

_____

_____

_____

_____

_____

_____

_____

_____

_____

_____

_____

_____

_____

_____

_____

Devotion 83

King Solomon was established on the throne, and his great wisdom was now known thanks to the issue of the one baby that two women both claimed as their own. All of that done, we are then made privy to some of the people that the new king surrounded himself with.

1 Kings 4:1 *So king Solomon was king over all Israel.* **2** *And these were the princes which he had; Azariah the son of Zadok the priest, 3 Elihoreph and Ahiah, the sons of Shisha, scribes; Jehoshaphat the son of Ahilud, the recorder.* **4** *And Benaiah the son of Jehoiada was over the host: and Zadok and Abiathar were the priests:* **5** *And Azariah the son of Nathan was over the officers: and Zabud the son of Nathan was principal officer, and the king's friend:*

In this list, we find priests, scribes, warriors, record keepers, officers...

And a friend.

Zabud, the principal officer, was also "the king's friend." This is the only time this man is ever even mentioned in the Bible, and he was mentioned in the context of being a friend to the king.

What better thing could any of us ever aspire to be? When it comes to our King, Jesus, not everyone is called to the ministry, not everyone is placed in some official position or office, but each and every one of us can be a friend to the King. In John 15:15 Jesus looked at His followers and said, "but I have called you friends..."

Each and every day, DO be a true friend to Jesus your king!

Personal Notes:

_____
_____
_____
_____
_____
_____
_____
_____
_____
_____
_____
_____
_____
_____
_____
_____
_____
_____
_____
_____
_____
_____
_____
_____
_____
_____
_____
_____

Devotion 84

For twenty-eight verses, 1 Kings 4 has listed for us the men, wealth, and wisdom of Solomon. But in verse twenty-nine one other thing is added for our notice.

1 Kings 4:29 *And God gave Solomon wisdom and understanding exceeding much, and largeness of heart, even as the sand that is on the sea shore.*

Largeness of heart. It means the exact same thing as when we today say, "So and so has a big heart." Solomon was not just smart and successful; he put his heart into everything he did and everyone he met. Ruling the people and serving the Lord were not just duties or rituals to him. In these early years, when he was right with God, he did all that he did from the heart, and everyone could see it.

It is very easy, as we grow in our knowledge of Scripture, to become cold, and even a bit haughty. It is easy to begin to be puffed up in pride, and aloof from those who "are not on our level."

And each and every time we do so, no matter how much of a "big brain" we are demonstrating, we are also demonstrating a very small heart.

DO be very "large-hearted" to everyone around you, each and every day. The old statement "nobody cares how much you know until they know how much you care" is an accurate statement!

Personal Notes:

_____
_____
_____
_____
_____
_____
_____
_____
_____
_____
_____
_____
_____
_____
_____
_____
_____
_____
_____
_____
_____
_____
_____
_____
_____
_____
_____

Devotion 85

In the last five verses of 1 Kings 4, a catalog of some of Solomon's wisdom is given.

1 Kings 4:30 *And Solomon's wisdom excelled the wisdom of all the children of the east country, and all the wisdom of Egypt.* **31** *For he was wiser than all men; than Ethan the Ezrahite, and Heman, and Chalcol, and Darda, the sons of Mahol: and his fame was in all nations round about.* **32** *And he spake three thousand proverbs: and his songs were a thousand and five.* **33** *And he spake of trees, from the cedar tree that is in Lebanon even unto the hyssop that springeth out of the wall: he spake also of beasts, and of fowl, and of creeping things, and of fishes.* **34** *And there came of all people to hear the wisdom of Solomon, from all kings of the earth, which had heard of his wisdom.*

Note first of all that specific names of other men are given against which Solomon was compared. The Bible lists tens of thousands of names that people in those days actually knew! The Bible is not fiction, it is history, and in those days, it was easily verifiable history.

But what I really want you to see is that Solomon's wisdom was not merely theological. He also spoke 3,000 proverbs, many of which are utterly practical, he wrote one thousand and five songs, meaning he studied music, he studied and taught about trees and bushes, demonstrating a good understanding of botany, and he also lectured on animals, fish, and birds, showing good scholarship in zoology.

That ought to light a fire under all of us to do more than just "be ignoranter and ignoranter" for the Lord, as I heard a very painful to listen to preacher once say.

DO study your Bible. But DO also study history and math and biology and botany and zoology and geology and astronomy and any of a thousand other things that relate to the world our God has made, and the truth that He has established. People flocked from everywhere to hear Solomon simply because he had something wise to say! If he had been content to sink to the level of the "ignoranter and ignoranter" crowd, people would never have even crossed the street to hear him.

Personal Notes:

_____

_____

_____

_____

_____

_____

_____

_____

_____

_____

_____

_____

_____

_____

_____

_____

_____

_____

Devotion 86

In 1 Kings 5, Solomon was wealthy, wise, popular, and people were coming from everywhere to listen to him. But when Hiram, king of Tyre, sent a greeting to him, Solomon demonstrated yet another magnificent quality.

1 Kings 5:2 *And Solomon sent to Hiram, saying,* **3** *Thou knowest how that David my father could not build an house unto the name of the LORD his God for the wars which were about him on every side, until the LORD put them under the soles of his feet.* **4** *But now the LORD my God hath given me rest on every side, so that there is neither adversary nor evil occurrent.* **5** *And, behold, I purpose to build an house unto the name of the LORD my God, as the LORD spake unto David my father, saying, Thy son, whom I will set upon thy throne in thy room, he shall build an house unto my name.* **6** *Now therefore command thou that they hew me cedar trees out of Lebanon; and my servants shall be with thy servants: and unto thee will I give hire for thy servants according to all that thou shalt appoint: for thou knowest that there is not among us any that can skill to hew timber like unto the Sidonians.*

It is that last phrase that is so impressive in all of this: "thou knowest that there is not among us any that can skill to hew timber like unto the Sidonians." This was Solomon saying, "Hiram, I am wealthy and wise and successful, and my kingdom is powerful and full of great people, but there is absolutely none of us in this entire kingdom as good at hewing timbers as you Sidonians."

It is called humility. Solomon freely acknowledged an area in which others were superior to him and his people.

DO strive to be successful for the glory of God. But no matter how successful you ever get, DO be humble. No one can do everything, and those who are humble attract the needed help that the proud foolishly push away!

Personal Notes:

_____

_____

_____

_____

_____

_____

_____

_____

_____

_____

_____

_____

_____

_____

_____

_____

_____

_____

_____

_____

_____

_____

_____

Devotion 87

In 1 Kings 5:6, Solomon had asked for cedar timbers, and people to hew them properly for the building of the temple in Jerusalem. He had also promised to pay the hewers. Here is how Hiram responded.

1 Kings 5:8 *And Hiram sent to Solomon, saying, I have considered the things which thou sentest to me for: and I will do all thy desire concerning timber of cedar, and concerning timber of fir.* **9** *My servants shall bring them down from Lebanon unto the sea: and I will convey them by sea in floats unto the place that thou shalt appoint me, and will cause them to be discharged there, and thou shalt receive them: and thou shalt accomplish my desire, in giving food for my household.*

Both King Solomon and King Hiram had, in their words, "desires." Solomon desired timbers, and Hiram in verse nine said that his desire was "food for his household," and by household, he meant all of his servants.

This tells us that these two kings and kingdoms were in different situations at the moment. No one in Solomon's household was concerned about food. But in Hiram's household, they were. So Solomon's situation was one of wealth and ease, and Hiram's situation was one of need and struggle.

And yet verse twelve lets us know that these men and their kingdoms became friends.

That is a good lesson for Christians today. DO refuse to seek out friends based on wealth and status! Jesus left heaven's glory and splendor and became friends with people who were poor, struggling, and needy, and in so doing, He changed those friends for the better forever.

Personal Notes:

_____

_____

_____

_____

_____

_____

_____

_____

_____

_____

_____

_____

_____

_____

_____

_____

_____

_____

_____

_____

_____

_____

_____

_____

_____

_____

_____

Devotion 88

All of 1 Kings 6 describes the temple of the Lord that Solomon built. It was a truly magnificent structure:

1 Kings 6:27 *And he set the cherubims within the inner house: and they stretched forth the wings of the cherubims, so that the wing of the one touched the one wall, and the wing of the other cherub touched the other wall; and their wings touched one another in the midst of the house.* **28** *And he overlaid the cherubims with gold.* **29** *And he carved all the walls of the house round about with carved figures of cherubims and palm trees and open flowers, within and without.* **30** *And the floor of the house he overlaid with gold, within and without.* **31** *And for the entering of the oracle he made doors of olive tree: the lintel and side posts were a fifth part of the wall.* **32** *The two doors also were of olive tree; and he carved upon them carvings of cherubims and palm trees and open flowers, and overlaid them with gold, and spread gold upon the cherubims, and upon the palm trees.*

Gold, gold, gold everywhere, even the floors were covered in gold! Solomon went all out in building the house of God.

Is there any applicable parallel to the church today? Yes and no. Remember that in that day, that temple was the one and only house of worship for everyone in the entire nation. In a situation like that, gold on the floor makes some sense!

In the days of the New Testament, though, God established churches all over the place, not simply one place per nation. Still, while gold on the floor would clearly be extravagant, there is even today a good balance to be struck between frugality and finery in the house of God. We do not ever want to be so extravagant as to appear wasteful with the resources God gives us, but neither do we want to be so cheap as to send the message that we believe in "junk for Jesus."

DO value the house of God; it is where we meet as a body to worship Him. And even though we do not, and never will have "gold floors" (or even gold faucets) DO treat the house of God as the very special place that it still is!

Personal Notes:

_____

_____

_____

_____

_____

_____

_____

_____

_____

_____

_____

_____

_____

_____

_____

_____

_____

_____

_____

_____

Devotion 89

In 1 Kings 7, we see Solomon the builder. This single chapter describes his building of the Temple, his own house, a house for Pharaoh's daughter whom he married, and another house called the House of the Forest of Lebanon. All of it was utterly spectacular. In some of the particular details given, though, we find not just physical treasure but spiritual treasure as well.

1 Kings 7:13 *And king Solomon sent and fetched Hiram out of Tyre.* **14** *He was a widow's son of the tribe of Naphtali, and his father was a man of Tyre, a worker in brass: and he was filled with wisdom, and understanding, and cunning to work all works in brass. And he came to king Solomon, and wrought all his work.* **15** *For he cast two pillars of brass, of eighteen cubits high apiece: and a line of twelve cubits did compass either of them about.*

1 Kings 7:24 *And under the brim of it round about there were knops compassing it, ten in a cubit, compassing the sea round about: the knops were cast in two rows, when it was cast.*

1 Kings 7:37 *After this manner he made the ten bases: all of them had one casting, one measure, and one size.*

In all three of those passages, we see Hiram, Solomon's builder, using casting as his methodology. It is still used in jewelry and other metalwork to this very day. A mold is made, metal is melted, and then is poured into that mold. The mold is then removed, leaving the metal product.

And that is much like how God forms us into His own image. The Bible is the mold, and as we allow God to soften and melt us, the Word forms us into the product God is after.

DO allow God to soften you and pour you into that mold; the finished product He has in mind will be worth the heat we go through along the way!

Personal Notes:

_____

_____

_____

_____

_____

_____

_____

_____

_____

_____

_____

_____

_____

_____

_____

_____

_____

_____

_____

_____

_____

_____

_____

_____

_____

_____

_____

Devotion 90

Solomon had spent seven years building the Temple, the House of God. It was large... it was ornate... it was expensive... and it was meaningless because it was empty of the one thing that mattered.

1 Kings 8:1 *Then Solomon assembled the elders of Israel, and all the heads of the tribes, the chief of the fathers of the children of Israel, unto king Solomon in Jerusalem, that they might bring up the ark of the covenant of the LORD out of the city of David, which is Zion.*

David had lived in southwest Jerusalem, and that portion became known as the city of David. The temple was built on Mount Moriah on an elevation in the eastern part of the city. The Ark of the Covenant was still sitting in the tabernacle, the simple tent that David had prepared for it. All the way across town there was a brand new shiny temple, incomparable in worth, yet devoid of the presence of God.

Solomon knew this. The entire building project had been about this, in fact. And so in 1 Kings 8:1, he set the wheels in motion to bring the Ark of God from the tent to the Temple. No matter how ornate and expensive the structure, if there is no power and presence of God in it, it is empty and useless.

DO apply that truth to your home, your church, your life. No matter how grand any of those things look, no matter how expensive or expansive, DO seek the power and presence of God within them above all else!

Personal Notes:

_____
_____
_____
_____
_____
_____
_____
_____
_____
_____
_____
_____
_____
_____
_____
_____
_____
_____
_____
_____
_____
_____
_____
_____
_____

Devotion 91

1 Kings 8:6-9 gives us some fascinating details about the Ark of the Covenant when it was finally placed into the brand new Temple of Solomon.

1 Kings 8:6 *And the priests brought in the ark of the covenant of the LORD unto his place, into the oracle of the house, to the most holy place, even under the wings of the cherubims. 7 For the cherubims spread forth their two wings over the place of the ark, and the cherubims covered the ark and the staves thereof above. 8 And they drew out the staves, that the ends of the staves were seen out in the holy place before the oracle, and they were not seen without: and there they are unto this day. 9 There was nothing in the ark save the two tables of stone, which Moses put there at Horeb, when the LORD made a covenant with the children of Israel, when they came out of the land of Egypt.*

When verse eight tells us that the staves in the sides of the Ark were there "unto this day," it lets us know that the book of 1 Kings was written before the destruction of the temple at the hands of Nebuchadnezzar. But verse nine also says that the only thing actually inside the Ark was the two tables of stones containing the Ten Commandments. In other words, for all of the incredibly important things in the life and history of the Jewish nation, such as the pot of manna and Aaron's rod, which were put near the Ark inside the Most Holy Place, the only things ever allowed inside the Ark itself was that which was written by God, His Word. That alone was so utterly precious that God opened the lid to the Ark and said, "Put that in here."

Now you have some idea how God views the Bible, the written Word of God!

DO respect, revere, read, and retain God's Word. If it was the only thing ever allowed inside the Ark, it should be the primary thing taken into your heart!

Personal Notes:

_____

_____

_____

_____

_____

_____

_____

_____

_____

_____

_____

_____

_____

_____

_____

_____

_____

_____

_____

_____

_____

_____

_____

_____

_____

_____

Devotion 92

As the Ark was set in place and the priests came out of the Holy Place, they did so with the intention of "doing their job as ministers" on that day. They had done this job for many, many years with the Ark in the Tabernacle.

But on this special day, in this brand new house of God, the "usual service" was about to be completely interrupted.

1 Kings 8:10 *And it came to pass, when the priests were come out of the holy place, that the cloud filled the house of the LORD,* **11** *So that the priests could not stand to minister because of the cloud: for the glory of the LORD had filled the house of the LORD.*

Quite often in our day, rather than worshiping the Lord, people "worship their worship." They have everything planned, scheduled, choreographed, and rehearsed, so much so that the only "cloud that fills the house" is the cloud of their own pride, blinding their eyes to the fact that God is not in the house along with them.

If we truly worship the Lord, we should expect that there will be some times that we "cannot stand to minister" because the glory of God has filled the House. Our messages will go unpreached, our announcements ungiven, our schedules unfollowed, and yet we will leave saying, "It was good to be in the House of the Lord!"

DO come ready to worship each and every service. But DO remember to worship the Lord rather than worshiping your worship!

Personal Notes:

_____
_____
_____
_____
_____
_____
_____
_____
_____
_____
_____
_____
_____
_____
_____
_____
_____
_____
_____
_____
_____
_____
_____
_____
_____
_____
_____
_____
_____

Devotion 93

Having seen the glory of the Lord fill the Temple, Solomon, in the sight of all the people, began to pray. It was a long prayer, going from 1 Kings 8:23 to 1 Kings 8:53. And while what he spoke during that prayer was awe-inspiring, what he spoke without speaking was no doubt just as awe-inspiring to the people assembled that day.

Let me show you two verses and see if you figure out what I mean.

Here is Solomon as he starts to pray. **1 Kings 8:22** *And Solomon stood before the altar of the LORD in the presence of all the congregation of Israel, and spread forth his hands toward heaven:*

Here is Solomon as he finishes his prayer. **1 Kings 8:54** *And it was so, that when Solomon had made an end of praying all this prayer and supplication unto the LORD, he arose from before the altar of the LORD, from kneeling on his knees with his hands spread up to heaven.*

Do you see it?

When Solomon started to pray in the sight of all the people, he was on his feet. But by the time he ended that prayer in the sight of all the people, he was getting up off his knees. What must it have been like for the people to see their glorious king go down to his knees before God! What awe of God that must have inspired in them!

DO have a posture before God that inspires an awe of God in your children and in others as they watch you. They will learn as much or more from what they see you do than from what they hear you say!

Personal Notes:

Devotion 94

When Solomon finished praying, he stood to his feet and then turned to address the people of Israel. When he did, he said something very instructive.

1 Kings 8:55 *And he stood, and blessed all the congregation of Israel with a loud voice, saying,* **56** *Blessed be the LORD, that hath given rest unto his people Israel, according to all that he promised: there hath not failed one word of all his good promise, which he promised by the hand of Moses his servant.* **57** *The LORD our God be with us, as he was with our fathers: let him not leave us, nor forsake us:* **58** *That he may incline our hearts unto him, to walk in all his ways, and to keep his commandments, and his statutes, and his judgments, which he commanded our fathers.*

Notice that phrase, "That he may incline our hearts unto him." We so often pray as if we are trying to get God to "incline His heart to ours." Throughout Scripture, though, that is never the case. Anytime "heart" and "incline" go together, it is our heart to Him, never the other way around! His "ear" is often inclined to us, but the only heart that needs bending and moving is ours.

Solomon said, "That he may incline our hearts unto him, to walk in all his ways, and to keep his commandments, and his statutes, and his judgments, which he commanded our fathers." In other words, "Lord, help us to bow our wills and obey you!"

Now that is a prayer that God will always answer!

DO pray, every day, not that God's heart will incline to yours, but that your heart will incline to His!

Personal Notes:

_____
_____
_____
_____
_____
_____
_____
_____
_____
_____
_____
_____
_____
_____
_____
_____
_____
_____
_____
_____
_____
_____
_____
_____
_____
_____
_____
_____

Other Books by Dr. Bo Wagner

Beyond the Colored Coat
Daniel: Breathtaking
DO Drops (Vol. 1)
DO Drops (Vol. 2)
DO Drops (Vol. 3)
Don't Muzzle the Ox
Esther: Five Feast and the Fingerprints of God
From Footers to Finish Nails
I'm Saved! Now What???
James: The Pen and the Plumb Line
Jonah: A Study in Greatness
Marriage Makers/Marriage Breakers
Nehemiah: A Labor of Love
Romans: Salvation From A-Z
Ruth: Diamonds in the Darkness

Fiction Titles

The Night Heroes Series:
Cry From the Coal Mine (Vol. 1)
Free Fall (Vol. 2)
Broken Brotherhood (Vol. 3)
The Blade of Black Crow (Vol. 4)
Ghost Ship (Vol. 5)
When Serpents Rise (Vol. 6)
Moth Man (Vol. 7)
Runaway (Vol. 8)
Terror by Day (Vol. 9)

Sci-Fi

Zak Blue and the Great Space Chase:
Falcon Wing (Vol. 1)